NATURAL MEALS
IN
MINUTES

by Rita Bingham

with introduction by
Bob Moore of Bob's Red Mill, Milwaukie, Oregon

Published by *Natural* Meals Publishing

Natural Meals In Minutes introduces quick, easy recipes using time-proven, basic foods.... Grains, Legumes, Vegetables and Fruits, which are very low in fat (usually only 2-3%) and cholesterol-FREE.

With these unique techniques and nutritious recipes, you can make delicious meals from NATURAL foods in 30 minutes or less.

ISBN 1-882314-09-3

$14.95

Originally published as the Natural Meals In Minutes series:
  Book 1 - *Introduction To Natural Foods*
  Book 2 - *Sprouting*
  Book 3 - *Powdered Milk Cheeses*

Published by Natural Meals Publishing
Internet: www.naturalmeals.com
E-mail: info@naturalmeals.com
  OR sales@naturalmeals.com
Fax: 405.359.3492
Order Line: 1.888.232.6706

Printed in United States of America

Cover Photo by Bozarth Photography, Guthrie, OK

NATURAL MEALS
IN
MINUTES

by Rita Bingham

**In just 30 minutes, you'll have
Great Low Fat Meals you can eat to your heart's content...
from Family Fare to Classic Cuisine**

Dedicated to my mother, Esther Dickey, who has spent a lifetime making the effort to reverse the trend toward the overuse of commercially prepared foods. For many years, she traveled the world, sharing her knowledge and preparing thousands of nutritious, low-cost "healthy" foods for countless groups of people interested in taking responsibility for their health and well-being. Her books, Passport To Survival and Skills For Survival have been read and used by hundreds of thousands of people seeking better health, better preparedness skills, and a sense of well-being that comes as we learn to properly feed and care for our bodies, giving thanks to God for the abundant blessings of this life.

Thanks also to:
My husband, Clair, for his great artwork to "lighten" up this book, and to our 5 beautiful children, who cheerfully (most of the time) tasted and commented on my experiments. They even provided enthusiastic encouragement, even when they would really rather not have one more new recipe. Kimm, now 14 and my last child left in the nest, has been my most valuable critic because she is not afraid to be honest with me. When she says a recipe is good, I KNOW it's something teenagers will enjoy. At times, she takes over a large part of the kitchen responsibilities, thus allowing me time to complete my writing projects;

The many willing people who have helped to find answers to my endless questions and tasted bazillions of samples created in developing 3-minute powdered milk cheeses, "cheeseburger" (a meat-textured product from powdered milk), 3-minute bean flour soups (especially the great people at Bob's Red Mill), and many other "firsts" that are presented in this book;

Dr. Lynn Ogden of the Food Science and Nutrition Department and Dr. Laren Robison of the Agronomy Department at Brigham Young University, for the technical information I needed to develop the recipes for 3-minute cheeses and bean flour soups.

About the Author

Since 1966, Rita Bingham has taught and encouraged healthy eating, carrying on the tradition of her mother, Esther Dickey who over 30 years ago wrote Passport to Survival (a comprehensive guide to using and storing basic foods), and Skills for Survival (a self-sufficiency manual of basic skills for surviving major and minor disasters).

Continuing in the tradition of her nutrition-oriented family, Rita uses wholesome, basic foods and imaginative techniques to create fast, high fiber recipes for every meal of the day, even snacks and desserts! Her husband and 5 children, as well as thousands of seminar participants, have given Rita's recipes rave reviews.

Rita has written a series of books on healthful eating; produced a training video to demonstrate some of the many ways nutritious foods can be prepared with a minimum amount of time; written articles for newspapers and magazines; co-hosted radio shows providing information and recipes for healthy eating. She has consulted for companies to help solve their food problems and create marketable products. She has also provided training on how to include nutritious foods in weight loss programs.

Across the U.S. and Canada, Rita has educated and encouraged companies to market Bean, Pea and Lentil Flours to create no-fat-added 3-minute soups, sauces and gravies. These flours can also be used in all types of breads, as well as in many other recipes. Bob's Red Mill (5209 S. E. International Way, Milwaukie, Oregon 97222, 503-654-3215) mills and markets these versatile flours.

Bean flours are now making their way into commercial products. Restaurants are now using these flours in recipes from home-style to gourmet. Rita also encourages the use of 3-minute bean flour soups in programs to feed the hungry in the U.S. and abroad.

Introduction

To YOUR GOOD HEALTH

For over 25 years I have enjoyed the challenge and romance of milling whole grain flours, meals and cereals on 100-year-old stone grinding mills. These simple and durable machines with their quartz stones have been grinding the world's food since Biblical times.

In these many years I have been miller, salesman, entrepreneur, president and leader of a whole grain natural foods company with national distribution, I can't remember anyone more dedicated to declaring the value of whole grains and legumes than Rita Bingham. Even more impressive is her talent and expertise in teaching others through her cookbooks, cooking demonstrations and talks on grains, beans, peas and lentils.

My staff and I had the privilege of joining her energy and talent together with our own several years ago. Rita came to us with her idea for milling and packaging bean, pea and lentil flours (with all the germ and fiber left in for that whole food goodness). Using our historical mill stones for grinding, we put out a line of these flours, now available in many stores throughout the country and by mail order from the mill. Our all natural, whole grain, bean, pea and lentil products are dedicated "To Your Good Health".

Now days, it's no secret that a diet consisting mainly of refined, over-processed foods is bad for your health. Nearly every magazine and newspaper is filled with findings of scientists who believe these foods weaken our immune systems, increase the risk of some forms of cancer, heart disease and other chronic diseases and decrease our natural energy levels. For years advertising has lured us toward these "fast" foods. As a result, we are eating more fat and almost no fiber. We weigh more and exercise less and we rely more on medicines to make us feel well. We need to turn back to basics like whole, cracked and ground grains and legumes.

Rita Bingham's "Natural Meals In Minutes" certainly starts us back, and "Country Beans" leaves us with no excuse but to begin on the path to good health by following her road map.

Bob Moore

Bob's Red Mill Natural Foods
Milwaukie, Oregon 97222

Foreword

Meals In Minutes - A step toward WELLNESS

Wellness is something everyone desires. We are bombarded daily by "fountain of youth" pills or potions...something to make us slim and trim, to give us more energy, to take away our aches and pains, to be able to work harder, faster, smarter. Are pills and potions the answer, or have we been blessed with the natural resources our bodies need in a more simple form? Most people think wellness has everything to do with being thin. Why is it then that some people can carry extra pounds and feel "well" their whole lives while many thin people suffer from an endless string of health problems?

While excess weight is definitely hard on the body, some bodies are able to handle the extra pounds better than others. Why? It is because some are blessed with stronger bodies than others; some have inherently strong immune systems; some have both, but most of us have an average amount of both. It takes a lot of effort to maintain the level of wellness we're born with and even more to improve on it.

With today's busy lifestyle, who has time? We all have the *same* amount of time. It is up to each one of us to decide how well we will care for the bodies we've been given. We have an obligation to feel our best so we can live up to our potential, each doing our part to make this world a better place in which to live. Since the purpose of this book is to help busy cooks make healthy meals in a hurry, I won't go into the other areas of achieving wellness except to present a quick outline of what it takes to get on the right path. Much is written about each of the areas that make up wellness and each is equally important. Without paying attention to ALL the following areas, you will find yourself out of balance and feeling less than your best, because wellness is balance.

Wellness is about finding out how to choose wisely the things we become involved in and putting the rest on the back burner and eliminating excess "should do's" all together. (Most of my life, I didn't know it was alright to HAVE back burners, and now I keep losing them!)

Take the time to take care of yourself. No one else is going to do it for you! It's taken me 50[+] years to learn that I am worth the effort it takes to take care of my body. I hope this knowledge comes easier to you. If not, start now and learn to evaluate what your body needs to feel "WELL."

WELLNESS

5 important steps to achieving better health

1. Healthy Eating - Eating the best foods available (whole grains, beans, seeds, vegetables and fruits), with as much "live" (raw) food as possible, especially delicious, nutritious sprouts; limiting fats and refined foods; regulating the amount of food eaten to the amount of energy needed.

2. Exercise - Walking, 20-30 minutes a day, 5 days a week, combined with stretching any and all tense, tight muscles.

3. Positive Thinking - Replacing "can't," "shouldn't," "ought to," or "afraid to" with positives. Our minds are marvelous at obeying our commands, but most of our commands are negative. If we tell ourselves how fat we are, how sick we are, how depressed we are, our minds will obey and we WILL be. If we tell ourselves how healthy and strong we are, that we are able to think quickly and clearly, that our immune system is growing stronger each day, etc., those things will come to pass!

4. Low Stress - We all need stress, but when daily stress wears us down rather than invigorates us, it becomes negative stress. Breathing becomes shallow, upsetting the body's oxygen balance. The immune system breaks down. Muscles become tense and tight, thereby restricting the flow of blood and causing soreness and additional tension...a vicious cycle that sets in motion a chain of events leading to illness.

5. Righteous Living - Everyone needs the support of believing in a higher being who created us, loves us, knows our needs and answers our prayers. We all have a need to be loved and we never feel more loved than when we give love away through service and genuinely caring for others. We are being watched over and protected. The challenges we are given are meant to strengthen us. We can and will feel at peace when we learn to accept what we are given and make the best of it.

Table of Contents

The Basic Ingredients

BASIC FOODS with basic flavorings produce *amazingly good* basic meals! In the interest of good health, my goal has always been to make fast, interesting meals with as many nutritious, low-fat, wholesome ingredients as possible (and still have teenagers enjoy eating at home). Like a basic sewing pattern where you add trimmings to suit your taste, this book is meant to help you get acquainted with basic foods so you can prepare them quickly and enjoy serving them at every meal. Then you can easily adjust the recipes to include the ingredients (trimmings) you have on hand. A well-stocked healthy pantry should include at least a four-week supply of the ingredients used in this book. In addition, include lots of fresh fruits and crunchy veggies (at least 5 servings per day).

WHEAT, the staff of life, is indeed a versatile grain. Used in appetizers, main dishes, salads, snacks and desserts, wheat adds flavor, texture, and protein as well as many important vitamins and minerals. Fiber in the American diet is a popular subject these days, and whole wheat is one of the best tasting and easiest to use sources of fiber available. Cracked wheat cooks in only 15 minutes and can be added to almost any recipe.

If you are just beginning to use high-fiber whole grains, start by including small quantities of cracked wheat or whole wheat flour each day in your diet, as large quantities of fiber foods can cause diarrhea.

Many people are becoming allergic to wheat. Whether this is because of the frequency of use, the many chemicals used in crop production, or because of some other undiscovered cause is not clear. Many people who have experienced strong reactions to wheat have found that they can tolerate sprouted wheat. Sprouting increases the enzymes necessary for digestion, so it is a possibility that some food allergies are related to an insufficient quantity of digestive enzymes.

Food Allergies: The best way to avoid food allergies of all types is to practice a 4-day rotation plan, using the foods most likely to cause an allergic reaction only every 4th day and only in small quantities. (These foods are: milk, eggs, wheat, soy and corn.)   It also makes good sense to use sprouts, unprocessed whole grains, and organically grown foods whenever possible. Most people, after following this type of diet for a few weeks, find they can better tolerate the offending foods when eating out or with friends or when they just can't stand being so regimented for even one more MINUTE!

Many who are allergic to wheat can easily tolerate rice. While it is always best to use whole grains (as in brown rice), those unused to whole grain fiber may need to start by using white rice, then mixing in quantities of brown rice, gradually eliminating white rice. Brown Basmati rice is our family favorite—even for those who used to like only white rice.   Like cracked wheat, cracked rice takes only 15 minutes to cook, even for long grain rice that traditionally takes 45 minutes to cook. Rice can be used in any recipe calling for whole or cracked wheat.

Triticale, spelt and kamut are all members of the wheat family, but are often tolerated by those allergic to wheat and can be used in place of wheat in any recipe. Barley, also an excellent source of nutrition and fiber, can be substituted in some recipes. It is a great addition to any soup.

When a recipe calls for wheat flour, a Gluten-Free (GF) flour mixture may be substituted.   (Usually, extra leavening in the form of eggs or egg substitutes are added to replace the gluten found in wheat.)   I find the commercial varieties very white, processed-tasting and pasty, so I have developed my own "healthy" mix using brown rice flour, whole bean flour and other ingredients. See index for the GF Flour Mix recipe, or purchase GF Flour at your favorite health food store.

DRY BEANS (LEGUMES) are one of the best food bargains on the grocery shelves. Beans, peas and lentils are important staple foods for well over half the world's population. Many of us in the United States are just now learning to appreciate their hearty goodness. Most of us are familiar with pinto and kidney beans and homemade split pea soup, but there are many other, almost limitless ways to use legumes.

Legumes are born mixers as well as meat extenders. They can be mixed with other vegetables, used to "beef" up a salad, or served as dips and sandwich spreads. Legumes are a rich source of protein, iron, calcium, phosphorus, thiamin and potassium. When combined with grains, they supply all the amino acids necessary to form a complete protein.

Page 2

With advance preparat
Beans can be cooked, sp
frozen until ready for use

See COUNTRY BEANS for nea
recipes using bean flour, th
delicious, nutritious creamy
will also find nearly 300 fast
some, filling, meatless meals in

DRY MILK POWDER is inclu
non-instant milk, but any *powde*
instant milks with large crystals (l
a dry blender and process to a fin
make 1 gallon of milk. They can th
powder." Don't throw away "old m
perfect way to use old, slightly off-
rinsing and draining process washes a

HONEY is the most natural sweetene
sweetener, although sugar may be subst
ing conversion: 1 c. honey = 1 1/4 c. sug
been specially developed to use honey, ar
be made. Maple syrup can be used in pl
Note: Raw, unfiltered honey has been determ
year old.

be added to many last-minute meals;
or even ground to a fine flour; then
with nearly 120 fast, easy
in only 3 minutes for
free, of course!). You
beans for whole-

using

Sprouting
Heavy saucepan
Thermos - 1 q

HOW T

Cal. refers
Food Pyra
is for gr
about 1
Fat
tota

FLAVORINGS are an essential part of any natural food diet.
vegetable or meat based bouillon or soup bases, and other ordinary
spices and seasonings. (For a more complete list of the ingredients used in
book, see p. 177) Liquid extracts or oils like coconut, cherry, mint, strawberry,
etc., are compact and very helpful in making drinks, baked goods, etc., when
fresh fruits are not available. Dry seasoning mixes such as Italian, taco, barbecue
and enchilada are helpful, but not essential. All of these seasoning mixes can be
made at home without preservatives and with little or no salt. As you find
favorite recipes, buy and store quantities of your favorite herbs, spices, and flavorings to season them.

SKILLET COOKERY and "One Pot Meals" conserve time and energy. I've been
accused of cooking as if I only own one pot, so I try to live up to my reputation!
Many oven-baked recipes can be cooked in a skillet or dutch oven.

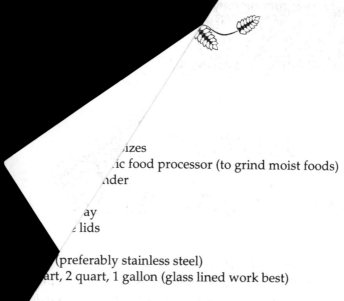

.izes

.ic food processor (to grind moist foods)

.nder

.ay

. lids

(preferably stainless steel)

.art, 2 quart, 1 gallon (glass lined work best)

READ THE NUTRITIONAL INFORMATION

Cal. 170 **Fat** .7g/4% **Carb** .30g **Fbr.** 6g **Pro.** 17g

to the number of calories in one serving. Even though the USDA .nid uses 2,000 calories per day as the "norm" for women, that figure .wing children and very active adults. Most women do very well on .200 calories per day from wholesome foods.

shows the grams of fat per serving, followed by the percentage of fat to . calories. Any product over 10% fat should be eaten sparingly. Most active .men maintain or lose excess pounds when they consume 20-25 grams of fat .er day. Active people burn more fat so they can get away with consuming more fat without gaining weight, but that doesn't mean they're "healthy." According to Dr. Dean Ornish and thousands of other physicians, a less than 10% fat diet is essential for regaining health and losing excess weight. The body actually needs very few added fats, as whole foods contain adequate amounts of fat for proper growth and nourishment.

Carb. gives the grams of carbohydrate available. Whole foods provide the best sources of quick energy, while maintaining stable blood sugar levels.

Fbr. refers to the grams of fiber, a very important ingredient in avoiding colon cancer and a host of other diseases and digestive problems.

Pro. gives the number of grams of protein in one serving. If you worry about adequate protein intake on a vegetarian diet, research has shown that it is impossible NOT to get enough protein when you use wholesome beans, grains, and leafy, green vegetables are eaten on a daily basis.

Introduction
To Natural Foods

Whole grains and legumes can be cracked or ground to a fine flour to reduce cooking time. Cracked grains cook in only 15 minutes and provide the basis for hundreds of delicious patties, cereals, breads, soups, salads, sandwich fillings, casseroles and even desserts. Beans and legumes ground to a flour cook in only 3 minutes to make good-for-you low-fat or no-fat creamy soups, sauces and gravies you can eat to your heart's content.

BREAKFASTS

For A Better Beginning

My family likes the satisfying feeling of having eaten a hearty, wholesome breakfast that eliminates the "hungries" that attack several hours after a skimpy breakfast of processed cold cereal. Wholesome, nutritious foods satisfy longer and for us, are infinitely more exciting.

CRACKED WHEAT CEREAL

1 3/4 c. water   *1 c. cracked wheat*

To obtain fluffy, individual grains, home-cracked wheat (or brown rice) will need to be sifted to remove the flour and very fine grain particles.* Salt can be added after cooking. Cracked wheat cooked in this way will be used in many recipes in this book.

Put water and wheat (or brown rice) into heavy saucepan. Bring to a full boil, cover, turn off heat and let sit 15 min., or until water is absorbed. Flavor, vitamins and fluffy texture are retained when heat is kept below boiling. If you prefer "mush," simmer for 15 minutes. Serve hot with milk and honey.   Serves 4.

To save for use in other recipes, package cooked wheat or brown rice in 2-cup portions in zip-loc bags. Flatten to force out air. Freeze for up to 3 months.

(To cook without electricity: In a heated 1 qt. thermos, add boiling water to dry cracked rice or wheat and seal container. Lay thermos on its side and "cook" for 20-30 minutes.)

*These very fine grain particles are called "Farina" and are like Cream of Wheat® or Cream of Rice®. See following recipe for "Creamy Wheat Cereal."

Cal. 28 **Fat** .2g/7% **Carb.** 6.5g **Fbr.** 8g **Pro.** 1g

FARINA

Farina is very finely cracked grain, usually rice or wheat. When I sift cracked grains, I end up with 3 products: coarse cracked grain; farina; coarse flour. I use the coarse cracked grain for cereals, salads, sandwich fillings and pilaf, add the flour to breads and use the farina for cereal, or in breads and muffins.

Using a grain cracker, spice mill or blender, coarsely crack wheat or rice kernels. (Electric flour mills generally cannot be set coarse enough to produce a good farina.) Sift, using a coarse then a fine strainer to separate farina from flour. Use within 1 month, or refrigerate in an airtight container.

CREAMY WHEAT CEREAL

2/3 c. farina   *3 1/4 c. hot water*
1/4 c. dry milk powder (opt.)

Microwave:
Stir all ingredients in a 6-cup microwave bowl. Cook on high for 1 minute. Stir
well. Cook 2-3 minutes more until cereal thickens, stirring every 30 seconds.
Stir. Let stand to desired consistency.

Stovetop:
Heat water to boiling. Gradually stir in combined farina and milk (if used).
Cook 2 minutes, stirring occasionally. Remove from heat and cover. Let stand 2
minutes before serving.

Season with honey or maple syrup. Serve with milk or milk substitute. Serves 4.

Cal. 122 **Fat** .5g/4% **Carb.** 25g **Fbr.** 1g **Pro.** 5g

STEAMED WHEAT OR RICE

4 c. whole wheat or brown rice   *4 c. water*

Put the wheat or rice and water in a 3 qt. glass or metal bowl and set inside a 6
qt. pan filled with 2" of water. Put a canning jar ring or metal kitchen utensils
between pans to keep the grains pan from touching the bottom of the water pan.
Put lid on outer pan and bring water to a boil. Reduce heat and gently steam for
1 hour. The starch granules in the kernels of grain will swell or burst and completely absorb the water.

If you want grain that is easier to chew, use 4 c. grain and 8 c. water and steam
for 3-4 hours. This variation can be cooked overnight on low heat in a crock pot
or thermos for a delicious hot breakfast. Serves 6-8.

I like to freeze 2 cup quantities of cooked grains and beans in plastic zip-loc bags
to be thawed for use as cereal, in soups, casseroles, and patties. Flatten filled
bags so they will stack well.

Cal. 316 **Fat** 1.8g/5% **Carb.** 65g **Fbr.** 12g **Pro.** 14g

APPLE-CINNAMON OATMEAL

1 c. boiling water
1/8 c. dry apple dices or
1/2 c. grated fresh apple

2/3 c. rolled oats
1/4 t. vanilla
1/4 t. cinnamon

Add ingredients to boiling water. Bring back to a boil. Cover pan with a lid and turn off heat. Let sit 5 minutes, stirring once. Serve hot with milk, adding salt and sweetener to taste. Serves 2.

Cal. 109 **Fat** 1.7g/14% **Carb.** 19g **Fbr.** 3g **Pro.** 4g

HONEY MAPLE GRANOLA

7c. rolled oats
1 c. whole wheat flour
1/2 c. apple juice concentrate
1 c. honey, melted
1 t. ea. vanilla and mapleine
1/4 c. water or canola oil

1 c. chopped nuts (opt.)
1 c. grated coconut (opt.)
1 T. ground sunflower seeds (opt)
1 T. ground flax seeds (opt)
 grated rind of one lemon

Mix dry ingredients, then add honey, vanilla and mapleine, and water or oil. Mix well and spread out on baking sheets. Bake 2 hours at 150°F, stirring every half hour. Add 2 cups raisins or chopped dates, if desired, after baking. Makes about 1 gallon.

Note: *Adding seeds and nuts increases the fat content, but these are the fats we *should* be eating, and eliminating fatty meats, fried foods, and foods containing trans-fats. If desired, you may substitute canola oil for apple juice concentrate.

Cal. 132 **Fat** 2.8g/18% **Carb.** 25g **Fbr.** 3g **Pro.** 4g

MALT-O-NOLA

6 c. oatmeal
1 c. malted milk powder
1 c. dry milk powder
1/2 c. sesame seeds
1 c. chopped nuts (opt.)

3 c. wheat germ
3/4 c. hot water or canola oil
2 c. honey
grated rind of one lemon
1 t. vanilla

Mix dry ingredients. Make a nest and add water (or oil) mixed with honey, vanilla and lemon rind. Stir well and spread thin on baking sheets. Bake at 300°F 1-2 hours, stirring well, until dry and crunchy. Makes 14 cups.

Cal. 170 **Fat** 3.1g/16% **Carb.** 32g **Fbr.** 2g **Pro.** 6g

RAW WHEAT PANCAKES

For those without a grinder...

1 c. wheat kernels
1 T. canola oil (opt.)
2 eggs, separated

2 t. baking powder
1/2 t. salt
2 T. dry milk powder

Soak 1 c. whole wheat kernels overnight in 2 cups water. Drain, reserving 3/4 cup liquid. Beat whites separately. Add soaked wheat and reserved liquid to blender. Process on high until very smooth, about 2 minutes. Add egg yolks and dry ingredients. Pour batter into mixing bowl and fold in egg whites. Ladle onto hot griddle and cook until browned on both sides.

Cal. 156 **Fat** 4.6g/3% **Carb.** 23g **Fbr.** 4g **Pro.** 8g

FLUFFY BUTTERMILK PANCAKES

2 c. fine wheat flour
1/4 t. salt (optional)
1/4 c. dry milk powder
1 T. baking powder
1 3/4 c. warm water

1/2 c. buttermilk
1 T. honey
1 t. vanilla
2 T. applesauce or canola oil
4 egg whites, beaten stiff*

Stir dry ingredients well. Make a little "nest" in the flour mixture and add moist ingredients (except egg whites), stirring only until flour is moistened so the pancakes will be tender and light. Fold egg whites into batter. Ladle onto hot griddle or waffle iron and cook until brown on both sides. Try adding 1/2 t. ginger or allspice for variety. Serves 4 hungry kids.

*Note: If oil is added, use only 2 egg whites.

Cal. 264 **Fat** 1.3g/4% **Carb.** 53g **Fbr.** 7g **Pro.** 14g

WHEAT-FREE BUTTERMILK PANCAKES
Wheat and Gluten Free

1/3 c. tapioca flour
2/3 c. brown rice flour
1/3 c. white bean flour
1 t. baking powder
1/2 t. baking soda

1/2 t. salt
3/4 c. fresh buttermilk
1 T. honey
3 egg whites, beaten stiff (opt.)
2 T. canola oil (opt.)

Mix ingredients in order given, folding in egg whites last, if used. Pour 2" circles of batter onto griddle coated with cooking spray over medium-low heat. These require longer, slower cooking than wheat pancakes. Cook until golden brown on both sides.

*Note: If oil is added, use only 2 egg whites.

Cal. 184 **Fat** 1g/5% **Carb.** 34g **Fbr.** 3g **Pro.** 9g

GOLDEN GRAINS WAFFLE MIX
Wheat and Gluten-Free

1 c. tapioca flour
2 c. brown rice flour
1 c. white bean flour
3 T. sucanat or turbinado sugar

1 T. baking powder
1 1/2 t. baking soda
3/4 c. buttermilk powder

Keep in a cool place. To make pancakes or waffles for 4, combine:
1 1/2 c. dry pancake mix
1/4 t. vanilla
1 c. warm water

2 T. canola oil (opt.)
3 egg whites, beaten stiff

Mix all but egg whites for 30 seconds with whisk or on low speed with electric mixer. Fold in egg whites. Drop by tablespoon onto griddle lightly coated with cooking spray. Respray only as necessary. Cook until golden brown over medium-low heat, turning once. Serves 4.

*Note: If oil is added, use only 1 egg white.

Cal. 184 **Fat** 1g/5% **Carb.** 34g **Fbr.** 3g **Pro.** 9g

CINNAMON WHEAT-NUTS

3 c. whole wheat flour   *1 T. cinnamon*
1/2 t. salt   *3/4 c. buttermilk*
3/4 c. powdered honey or sucanat*   *1 T. vanilla*

Mix dry ingredients. Using electric mixer or egg beater, add buttermilk and vanilla and mix until you have very fine granules, just like commercial Grape Nuts. Spread on 2 or 3 baking sheets and bake at 325° for 10 minutes. Stir to break up granules and bake 5-10 minutes longer, until golden brown. Cool and store in air-tight container. Serve with hot or cold milk.

Cal. 217 **Fat.** 1.1g/1% **Carb.** 47g **Fbr.** 6g **Pro.** 7g

HONEY MAPLE-NUTS

3 c. whole wheat flour   *2 t. maple flavoring*
1/2 c. dry milk powder   *1/4 c. melted honey*
1/2 c. sucanat or powdered honey*   *6 T. water*
1/2 t. salt

Mix dry ingredients. Using electric mixer or egg beater, add maple flavoring, honey, and only enough water to moisten. Mixture should be very fine, just like commercial Grape Nuts. Spread on 2 or 3 baking sheets and bake at 325° for 10 minutes. Stir to break up granules and bake 5-10 minutes longer, until golden brown. Cool and store in air-tight container. Serve with hot or cold milk.

Cal. 150 **Fat.** 2g.11% **Carb.** 30g **Fbr.** 4g **Pro.** 6g

*Powdered honey is honey that is dried to a powder. It can be used in any recipe calling for sugar. Make sure the brand you buy is 100% honey, not a little honey and a lot of refined sugar! Powdered molasses is also available. A good source for both is Stillwater Ranch, P. O. Box 493583, Redding, CA 96049-3583. To order, call 1-800-429-1856

*Sucanat is granulated cane juice made from the sugar cane. Look for a brand that says it is made from unrefined cane juice.

See p. 49 in Quick Breads for great breakfast muffins!

SANDWICH
FILLINGS

SANDWICH FILLINGS can be made ahead for fast, nutritious lunches. I always have a good supply of either loaf bread, pita bread, crepes, or homemade wheat flour tortillas. Then, almost any leftover salad can be turned into a sandwich.

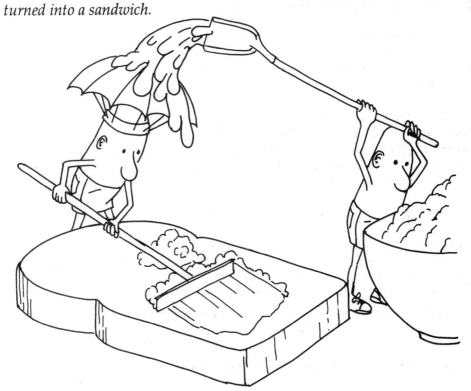

SEAFOOD SALAD FILLING

1/2 c. fat-free mayonnaise
1/4 c. catsup
1 large diced tomato
1/2 c. diced green pepper

1/2 c. diced green onions
6 1/2 oz. can drained tuna in water
2 c. cooked rice or cracked wheat
1/2 c. diced celery

Mix all ingredients well. Fill 6 pita pockets or use on toasted whole wheat bread.

Cal. 119 **Fat** .5g/4% **Carb.** 19g **Fbr.** 4g **Pro.** 10g

BURRITO OR TACO FILLING

1 c. cooked cracked wheat
1/4 t. cumin
1 T. parmesan cheese
salt to taste

1/2 c. cottage cheese
1 T. chopped green chilies
1/2 c. chopped onions
2 T. water

Put water and onions in heavy skillet and steam for 1 minute over medium-high heat. Add remaining ingredients and heat through. Use to fill flour tortillas, taco shells or pitas. Serves 4.

Cal. 71 **Fat** .6g/8% **Carb.** 12g **Fbr.** 2g **Pro.** 6g

WHEAT 'N CHEESE FILLING

1 t. chicken-flavored bouillon
1/2 c. diced celery
1/4 c. fat-free mayonnaise
1 c. cooked rice or cracked wheat

1/4 c. fat-free cottage cheese
2 chopped green onions
1 c. frozen peas, slightly thawed

Mix well and serve with lettuce on sliced bread or in pita pockets. Serves 4.

Cal. 88 **Fat** .3g/3% **Carb.** 17g **Fbr.** 4g **Pro.** 7g

HOT TUNA FILLING

6 1/2 oz. can drained tuna
2 T. fat-free mayonnaise
1 c. cooked rice or cracked wheat

1 c. fat-free cottage cheese
1 T. chopped green chilies
1/2 c. minced green onions

Place on top of lightly toasted pitas, wheat or rye bread and broil until bubbly. If desired, top each sandwich with 2 T. grated cheddar cheese before broiling. Also good wrapped in flour tortillas. Heat through and serve. Serves 4.

Cal. 86 **Fat** .3g/4% **Carb.** 8g **Fbr.** 2g **Pro.** 14g

SPICY VEGETABLE FILLING

1/2 large onion, chopped
1 large carrot, thinly sliced
1/8 t. garlic powder
1 t. chili powder
1/4 t. cumin

2 medium zucchini, cut in 1/2" cubes
1 large green or red bell pepper, chopped
1 c. whole kernel corn
1 c. cooked kidney or pinto beans
1 c. cooked brown rice

In a large skillet coated with cooking spray, stir-fry all ingredients over medium-high heat until mixture sizzles. Add 1/4 c. water to create steam and continue cooking until veggies are crispy-tender, adding additional water as necessary. Makes filling for 6 tacos or burritos, 12 Hot Pockets.

Hot Pocket Fillings (See p. 45 for Pocket Dough):

VEGGIE TACO FILLING

1 c. cooked Basmati rice
1/4 c. each grated onions,
carrots, cabbage
salt and pepper to taste

1/2 pkg. powdered taco seasoning
(or curry powder to taste)
1/2 c. fat-free cottage cheese

Mix well and spoon into hot pocket dough.

PIZZA FILLING

1 1/2 c. spaghetti sauce
1/4 c. chopped olives

2 c. fat-free cottage cheese
1/2 c. sliced mushrooms

Mix well and spoon into hot pocket dough. If desired, use grated mozzarella cheese in place of cottage cheese.

FRUIT FILLING

1 grated apple
1/2 t. vanilla

1 t. lemon juice
2 T. turbinado sugar or sucanat

Mix well and spoon into hot pocket dough. After baking, spread Fruit Hot Pockets with butter, then sprinkle with a cinnamon/sugar mixture.

SALADS

SALADS with wheat and vegetables can be used as a main dish for lunch or as a light supper. Most salads can be made ahead of time for especially busy days. Many leftover salads can be used as filling in pita pocket breads or rolled up in heated whole wheat flour tortillas. (See the breads section on p. 40)

TACO RICE SALAD

2 c. boiling water
1 c. brown rice
1 t. chili powder

1/2 t. salt
1/2 t. cumin

Add rice and seasonings to water and simmer until rice is tender. Time will vary according to the type of rice you use. Short grain rice is higher in starch and cooks faster. (I usually use cooked brown rice that has been frozen or refrigerated in 2-cup portions in zip-loc bags. To serve, heat bag of rice thoroughly in microwave or hot water.)

When rice is tender and cool, add:

1 c. cooked kidney beans
1/2 c. diced celery
1/2 t. cumin

1/2 c. fat-free cottage cheese
2 T. chopped onions
1/2 c. fat-free mayonnaise

Serve on a bed of lettuce and/or sprouts, topped with diced tomatoes. Sprinkle with grated cheddar cheese, if desired. Top with taco sauce and/or Ranch Dressing. Serves 4.

Cal. 170 **Fat** 1.1g/6% **Carb.** 33g **Fbr.** 3g **Pro.** 7g

GREEN PEA SALAD

16 oz. pkg. frozen petite peas
1 T. chopped green onions
3 chopped boiled eggs
1/8 t. prepared mustard

1 c. cooked rice or cracked wheat
2 T. chopped olives
1 T. chicken-flavored bouillon
2 T. fat-free mayonnaise

Put all into a bowl and mix well. This also makes a great Pita Pocket filling. Serves 6.

Cal. 101 **Fat** .9g/6% **Carb.** 20g **Fbr.** 6g **Pro.** 5g

QUICK GREEN BEAN SALAD

1 c. diced celery
3 c. green beans, cooked
1 4 oz. can chopped olives

2 tomatoes, diced
1/2 c. cooked rice or cracked wheat

Mix lightly and spoon onto serving plates. Top with Ranch Dressing. Add 1 T. Picante Sauce for a spicy-hot flavor. Serves 4.

Cal. 75 **Fat** 1g/11% **Carb.** 6g **Fbr.** 4g **Pro.** 3g

CREAMY CUCUMBER SALAD

2 c. cooked shell macaroni
2 T. chopped olives
2 T. Picante sauce
1/4 c. low-fat buttermilk

1 c. chopped cucumbers
1 diced tomato
1/4 c. fat-free mayonnaise
1/2 c. cooked rice or cracked wheat

Combine and mix lightly. Serve cold. Serves 6.

Cal. 100 **Fat** 1.1g/10% **Carb.** 20g **Fbr.** 3g **Pro.** 4g

ZUCCHINI-RICE SALAD

2 c. cooked brown rice or pasta
2 lg. tomatoes, diced
1 4 oz. can chopped olives

1 T. mild Picante sauce
2 c. grated zucchini
1/2 c. sliced mushrooms

Mix cooled rice or pasta with remaining ingredients. Serve plain or on lettuce-lined plates, topped with Buttermilk Dressing. If desired, sprinkle with toasted sunflower or sesame seeds and grated cheese. Serves 4.

Cal. 138 **Fat** 1.6g/10% **Carb.** 24g **Fbr.** 2g **Pro.** 4g

AVOCADO SALAD SUPREME

1 lg. avocado, diced*
1 c. frozen peas
2 T. chopped olives
1/2 t. chicken-flavored bouillon

2 T. mild Picante sauce
1/2 c. chopped celery
2 T. fat-free mayonnaise
1/2 c. cooked rice or cracked wheat

Mix all ingredients. Serve on lettuce lined plates garnished with fresh tomatoes and parsley or sprouts. This is also an excellent sandwich filling. Serves 4.

*Note: Although the fat content of avocadoes is high, they are a very valuable food, when used sparingly.

Cal. 145 **Fat** 8.1g/48% **Carb.** 16g **Fbr.** 5g **Pro.** 4g

CARROT-PINEAPPLE SALAD

1 1/2 c. cooked brown rice
1/2 c. crushed pineapple
1/2 c. fat-free mayonnaise

2 T. pineapple juice
1 1/2 c. shredded carrots
salt to taste

Mix chilled rice (or cracked wheat) with drained pineapple and add remaining ingredients. Serve in lettuce cups. If desired, top with raisins. Serves 4.

Cal. 150 **Fat** .8g/5% **Carb.** 2g **Fbr.** 3g **Pro.** 17g

DUTCH CUCUMBER SALAD

2 c. cooked rice or cracked wheat
1/4 c. minced green onions
1 c. fat-free cottage cheese

1 1/2 c. diced cucumbers
1/3 c. thinly sliced radishes
1/2 t. salt
1/8 t. pepper

Mix well and serve on a bed of lettuce or alfalfa sprouts, or as a pita bread filling.

Cal. 117 **Fat** .9g/7% **Carb.** .6g **Fbr.** 3g **Pro.** 7g

3 0076 00022 6419

DRESSINGS,
SAUCES
AND SPREADS

Rather than getting "bad press" for being high in fat, these recipes receive rave reviews. Most contain little or no fat. They are failproof and FAST. Use them to dress up your family favorites for company!

SALAD DRESSINGS are very easy to make, and lots more nutritious than commercial brands. Buttermilk Ranch Dressing is my most versatile favorite, as it is good not only on salads, but as a dip and moistening agent for sandwich fillings.

CREAMY RANCH DRESSING

2 c. fat-free mayonnaise
2 c. low-fat buttermilk
1/2 t. garlic powder
1 T. dried onion flakes

2 T. dried parsley
1/2 t. black pepper
1/2 to 1 t. salt

Put mayonnaise into a quart jar and stir while slowly adding buttermilk. When smooth, add remaining ingredients. Makes 1 quart. Note: Chives may be substituted for parsley. Variation: For **SPICY HOT DRESSING,** add 1/4 c. mild Picante sauce.

Cal. 15 **Fat** .1g/5% **Carb.** 3g **Fbr.** 0g **Pro.** 1g

CREAMY THOUSAND ISLAND DRESSING

1 c. fat-free mayonnaise
1/4 c. catsup

1 T. chopped dill pickles
dash Worcestershire sauce

Thoroughly mix mayonnaise, then stir in remaining ingredients. Serve cold.
Makes 1 1/4 cups.

Cal. 16 **Fat** .1g/5% **Carb.** 3g **Fbr.** 0g **Pro.** 1g

FRUIT SALAD DRESSING

2 T. frozen orange juice concentrate
1/4 c. fat-free mayonnaise
2 T. honey

1/4 c. yogurt
few drops vanilla

Blend and serve over mixed fruit salad. Makes 1/2 c. dressing.

Cal. 64 **Fat** 0g/.3% **Carb.** 15g **Fbr.** .1g **Pro.** 1g

SWEET AND SOUR SAUCE

1 c. pineapple juice　　　　*1 T. cornstarch*
2 t. molasses　　　　　　　*1 T. soy sauce*
1/2 c. honey　　　　　　　　*1/4 c. white vinegar*
1 medium bell pepper (green or red)

Finely chop bell pepper and simmer until tender in pineapple juice, molasses and honey. Mix remaining ingredients and add to juice mixture, stirring until thickened, about 1 minute. Makes 2 cups.

Cal. 127 **Fat** .1g/.4% **Carb.** 34g **Fbr.** .4g **Pro.** .5g

BLENDER WHITE SAUCE

3 T. unbleached flour　　　*1 c. boiling water*
2 T. dry milk powder　　　*1/2 t. salt*
3 T. butter or oil, (opt.)　　*dash pepper*

Blend all ingredients and cook over low heat 3 minutes, stirring occasionally. Makes 1 1/4 c. sauce. To make MOCK HOLLANDAISE SAUCE, blend in 2 egg yolks, 4 T. butter, and 1 T. lemon juice to cooked white sauce just before serving.

Cal. 19 **Fat** 0g/2% **Carb.** 3g **Fbr.** .6g **Pro.** 1g

PARMESAN CHEESE SAUCE

1/3 c. dry milk powder　　*1 egg yolk*
3 T. flour　　　　　　　　　*1/2 c. fat-free sour cream*
1/2 t. chicken bouillon　　　*2 T. butter or oil*
1 c. hot water　　　　　　　*1/4 c. Parmesan cheese*
salt and pepper to taste

Heat water to boiling. Blend dry milk powder, flour, bouillon, salt and water. Heat until thickened in saucepan. Blend remaining ingredients, adding half of the hot mixture gradually to egg mixture. Pour into saucepan and slowly heat until thickened. Blend again, if mixture curdles. Makes about 2 c. sauce.

Cal. 57 **Fat** 2.5g/43% **Carb.** 4g **Fbr.** 1g **Pro.** 3g

FAJITA SAUCE

2 T. cornstarch
1 t. beef bouillon
1 T. white vinegar
2 T. honey or sugar
2 c. water

1/4 c. soy sauce
1/4 t. powdered ginger
1/4 t. onion powder
1/4 t. garlic powder

Mix sauce ingredients and cook in a small saucepan over medium heat for 3 minutes. Makes 2 1/4 cups sauce.

Cal. 38 **Fat** 0g/0% **Carb.** 9g **Fbr.** .1g **Pro.** .3g

TOMATO-BASIL SAUCE

2 c. tomato sauce
1 T. pinto bean flour
4 t. chopped parsley
1/4 t. garlic powder

1 t. basil
1 t. oregano
dash white pepper
1 t. chicken-flavored bouillon

Mix sauce ingredients and cook in a small saucepan over medium heat until mixture is slightly thickened, then reduce heat to medium-low. Cover and cook 3 minutes. Makes 2 cups.

Cal. 25 **Fat** .2g/5% **Carb.** 6g **Fbr.** 1g **Pro.** 1g

DRY SAUCE MIX

This is a great sauce to use as a starter for cream soups and casseroles. Or, serve over pasta or rice.

2 c. non-instant dry milk powder
1/2 c. white bean flour
1/4 c. red lentil flour
1/2 c. cornstarch
1 T. dehydrated minced onion

3 T. chicken-flavored bouillon
1/4 t. dry mustard
1/4 t. leaf basil
1/4 t. white pepper
1/2 t. garlic powder

Combine all ingredients in 1-quart container. Cover tightly and stir or shake to mix. Store in a cool place and use within 6 weeks. Makes 3 cups.

Cal. 34 **Fat** .1g/2% **Carb.** 6g **Fbr.** 1g **Pro.** 2g

MUSHROOM SAUCE

2 c. water
2 t. beef bouillon
1 T. catsup
3 T. cornstarch

2 c. sliced fresh mushrooms
1/4 c. soy sauce
1/8 t. ginger

Mix all ingredients except cornstarch and cook in saucepan 3-5 minutes until mushrooms are tender. Mix cornstarch with 1/4 c. cold water, then stir slowly into hot mixture, adding only enough to thicken to desired consistency. Serve over meat, patties, rice, potatoes or other vegetables. (Reconstituted dried mushrooms can be used in place of fresh.) Makes 3 cups.

Cal. 39 **Fat** .1g/3.8% **Carb.** 6g **Fbr.** .4g **Pro.** 1g

FRUIT FLAVORED HONEY BUTTER

If you want a delicious spread for toast or pancakes in a variety of flavors, just add 1/8-1/2 t. of any of the following extract flavors to 1 c. honey and 3/4 c. butter and beat until fluffy:

Pineapple
Strawberry
Lemon

Coconut
Raspberry
Orange

Note. The amount of extract varies depending on the flavor of your honey and the type of flavoring you choose. You can also use some brands of powdered drink mixes in place of extracts. Makes 2 cups.

Cal. 47 **Fat** 2.8g/52% **Carb.** 6g **Fbr.** 0g **Pro.** 0g per T.

QUICK WHEAT OR RICE PATTIES

PATTIES are simple to make, quick to cook, and require only a mixing bowl, spoon, and a skillet. They can be served at any meal, plain or varied with toppings of cheese, sauces and gravies. Patties freeze well and can be thawed in the oven, microwave, toaster, or skillet.

Cracked wheat and brown rice form the basis of these high-fiber patties, with bean or lentil flour as a binder. As you become familiar with the texture required to form a good patty, you will be able to utilize foods on hand, including leftovers, to create your own delicious concoctions.

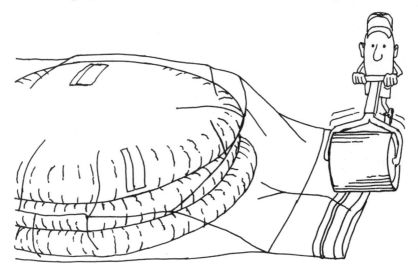

CRACKED WHEAT OR RICE PATTIES

2 c. cooked rice or cracked wheat
2 T. dry milk powder
4 egg whites or 2 eggs

1/2 c. chopped onion
1 T. dried parsley
2 t. chicken-flavored bouillon

Cracked wheat should be fairly dry and fluffy, like cooked rice. Mix all together. Drop by tablespoon onto skillet coated with cooking spray. Cover pan and brown on both sides over medium heat.

These are delicious hot or cold and are even better with a little salsa or grated cheese on top. These freeze well and can be eaten cold or reheated. This mixture could also be baked in a loaf pan or muffin tins until set at 350°F and served topped with mushroom soup or sweet and sour sauce. Serves 4-6.

Cal. 96 **Fat** .7g/6% **Carb.** 20g **Fbr.** 6g **Pro.** 6g

GRAIN AND GARDEN BURGERS

2 c. cooked brown rice
2 egg whites or 1 egg
1/4 c. grated onion
2 T. grated bell pepper

1/8 t. black pepper
2 T. red lentil flour
3/4 t. salt

Mix well. Place 1/4 c. of mixture in a skillet coated with cooking spray. Shape and flatten with a spatula. Cover pan and cook over medium-low heat until browned on both sides.

Serve plain or topped with white bean gravy, barbecue sauce, or cheese. OR, serve on a bun with all the fixin's. Serves 4.

Cal. 144 **Fat** 1.1g/6% **Carb.** 30g **Fbr.** 9g **Pro.** 7g

BROWN RICE BURGERS

1 c. cooked brown rice	*1 t. dry milk powder*
2 egg whites or 1 egg	*1/2 t. salt*
1/4 c. grated zucchini	*dash black pepper*
1/4 c. grated onion	*dash garlic powder*
1 t. white bean flour	*1 t. dried parsley*

Mix well. Drop by tablespoon onto skillet coated with cooking spray. Cover pan and cook over medium-low until browned on both sides. Serve plain, or top with White Bean Gravy.

For a real treat, serve with E-Z POTATO ROUNDS or SKINNY FRIES. See pp. 59 and 60. Serves 4.

Cal. 70 **Fat** .6g/6% **Carb.** 15g **Fbr.** 5g **Pro.** 4g

MINI WHEAT AND CHEESIES

2 eggs or 4 egg whites, beaten	*2 T. grated onion*
1 1/4 c. fat-free cottage cheese*	*1 c. water*
1/4 c. chopped green pepper	*1/4 c. dry milk powder*
1 t. chicken-flavored bouillon	*1 1/2 c. cooked rice or cracked wheat*

Preheat oven to 350°F. Add dry milk powder to rice or wheat and stir well, then add beaten eggs and stir again. Add remaining ingredients, mix, and pour into muffin tins coated with cooking spray, filled 3/4 full. Bake at 350°F 20-30 min.

*Grated cheddar cheese may be substituted for cottage cheese.

Note: These can also be cooked as a patty. Drop by tablespoon onto hot skillet coated with cooking spray and brown on both sides. Serves 6.

Cal. 127 **Fat** 1.8g/13% **Carb.** 16g **Fbr.** 1g **Pro.** 9g

FISH STICKS

2 c. cooked rice or cracked wheat	*2 T. cornstarch*
1 t. parsley or chives	*1 T. beef-flavored bouillon*
1 can undrained tuna fish in water	*1 c. bread crumbs or*
2 eggs	*parmesan cheese (for breading)*

Mix well. Press mixture 1/4" thick in flat pan containing 1/2 c. bread crumbs and/or parmesan cheese. Top with remaining mixture. Chill, slice into 1/2" strips and brown in a skillet coated with baking spray.

These can be frozen after cooking, like commercial fish sticks and then heated in an oven or a skillet. Serves 4-6.

Cal. 187 **Fat** 1.6g/8% **Carb.** 9g **Fbr.** 4g **Pro.** 14g

TACO PATTIES

1/2 t. cumin	*1 egg*
1/4 c. diced green chilies	*1/4 t. chili powder*
2 T. pinto bean flour	*2 t. beef-flavored bouillon*
2 t. dried parsley	*1 1/2 c. cooked rice or cracked wheat*

Mix all ingredients together. Drop by tablespoon onto hot skillet coated with cooking spray and brown on both sides.

Note: These can be cooked in muffin tins 3/4 full at 350°F for 20 minutes, then topped with grated cheese, if desired. Serves 4-6.

Cal. 72 **Fat** .5g/6% **Carb.** 14g **Fbr.** 1g **Pro.** 3g

MAIN DISH SOUPS

MAIN DISH SOUPS are fast, easy, nutritious, and provide a good opportunity to use up small amounts of leftover vegetables. The beans, rice, wheat, and peas in the recipes can be cooked, cracked, sprouted or ground ahead of time, then frozen, allowing you to prepare each recipe more quickly.

Cooking Without Electricity: *In times when electricity may not be available, the soups in this section could be put into a clean gallon jar or can with a tight-fitting lid and placed in a "nest" of crumpled newspapers, blankets, or clothing inside a cardboard box with a lid, such as an apple or orange box. When well insulated on all sides, raw wheat or brown rice and boiling water will "cook" in 10 hours.*

Thickening Soups: *Other countries use puréed vegetables to thicken their soups and stews. I like to use legume (bean, pea and lentil) flours as thickeners. Using any wheat grinder, dry legumes can be ground to a fine flour. These flours can be kept refrigerated or frozen for a quick, nutritious thickener. (2 T. flour thickens approximately 1 c. liquid.) (See* COUNTRY BEANS, *also by Rita Bingham, for nearly 400 bean recipes, including over 100 recipes using bean flours and instructions on how to grind and use a variety of flours.)*

CREAMY VEGETABLE SOUP

2 qt. boiling water
2 c. shredded potatoes
1/2 c. minced celery
1/2 c. shredded zucchini
1 t. dried parsley

3 T. chicken-flavored bouillon
1/2 c. minced onion
1 c. cooked rice or cracked wheat
1/2 c. dry milk powder
salt and pepper to taste (opt.)

Combine all ingredients except rice or wheat and dry milk. Cook about 15 minutes until potatoes are tender. Mix rice or wheat and dry milk together to prevent the powdered milk from lumping. Add the rice or wheat to the hot soup and stir well. Heat through and serve.

For variety, other fresh or frozen vegetables such as carrots, broccoli, peas or green pepper could be added. Serves 6.

Cal. 98 Fat .4g/4% Carb. 35g Fbr. 4g Pro. 6g

HEARTY CHILI

2 qt. tomatoes with juice
2 T. chili powder
1 lg. chopped green pepper
8 c. cooked kidney beans

3 T. cumin
1 lg. chopped onion
2 c. cooked rice
4 T. beef-flavored bouillon

Mix all ingredients together. Bring to a boil, then reduce heat to medium and cover pan. Cook over for an additional 15 minutes, stirring occasionally. This makes a good crock pot dinner. Serves 12.

Note: Cracked beans can be "cooked" in 8-10 hours in a thermos. Add 3 c. cracked beans to 6 c. boiling water. Bring back to a boil, then put into a gallon thermos. OR, bring to a boil in a covered saucepan, using 2 parts water to 1 part cracked beans, then cook over medium-low heat until tender, about 20 minutes.

Cal. 232 Fat 1.8g/7% Carb. 44g Fbr. 11g Pro. 13g

CHILI NOODLE SOUP

6 c. hot water
1 T. lemon juice
1 1/2 c. cooked black beans
1 1/2 c. cooked kidney beans
1 c. frozen corn
1 c. chopped mushrooms

1 c. macaroni noodles
1/2 c. chopped onions
1 t. cumin
4 T. green pea flour
2 T. chili powder
1/2 t. salt, or to taste

Mix all but flour and seasonings and bring to a boil. Whisk in seasonings. Reduce heat to low, cover pan and cook 15 minutes, stirring occasionally. Serves 8.

Cal. 160 **Fat** 1.1g/6% **Carb.** 31g **Fbr.** 5g **Pro.** 8g

"INSTANT" PEA SOUP

2 c. boiling water
3 T. pea flour (green or yellow)

2 t. chicken-flavored bouillon

Using dried peas (whole or split), grind them to a fine flour in a wheat mill. This flour can then ben frozen until ready for use. Mix bouillon with pea flour and whisk into boiling water. Cook over medium-high heat, stirring until thickened, about 1 minute. Reduce heat to medium-low, cover pan, and cook 2 minutes. Serve plain, or add cooked potatoes, carrots, celery and onions. Serves 2.

Cal. 20 **Fat** .1g/5% **Carb.** 4g **Fbr.** 1g **Pro.** 1g

MINESTRONE WITH RICE

3/4 c. sliced carrots
3/4 c. chopped onions
1 c. chopped celery
1 1/2 c. cabbage, coarsely chopped
4 c. water

5 beef-flavored bouillon cubes
1 c. canned tomatoes
salt and pepper to taste
1 1/2 c. hot cooked brown rice
1/4 c. Parmesan cheese (opt.)

Combine all ingredients except rice and cheese. Bring to a boil, cover, and simmer 20 minutes. Serve with a scoop of rice and sprinkle with Parmesan, if desired. Serves 4-6.

Cal. 85 **Fat** .6g/7% **Carb.** 18g **Fbr.** 2g **Pro.** 2g

CREAMY BEANS 'N RICE SOUP

4 c. hot water
2 c. cooked great northern beans
2 c. cooked brown rice
1/4 c. diced green pepper

1 c. diced onions
1 c. thinly sliced carrots
2 t. soy sauce
1/8 t. garlic powder
vegetable or chicken bouillon to taste

In 3 quart saucepan, cook all ingredients over medium-high heat for 5 minutes. Blend half of soup, in 1 cup batches, until smooth and creamy. Return to pan. Add 1 1/2 T. bouillon, or to taste. Serves 4-6.

Cal. 196 **Fat** 1g/4% **Carb.** 40g **Fbr.** 7g **Pro.** 9g

BROCCOLI STEM SOUP

What do you do with your leftover broccoli stems? Try them raw, add them to stir-fry, and use them in soups like this family favorite.

4 c. hot water
2/3 c. lima bean flour
1 c. peeled broccoli stems, diced

1/2 c. chopped onion
1/2 c. chopped carrots
4 t. vegetable bouillon, or to taste

Whisk bean flour into water. Add remaining ingredients. Cook over medium-high heat until veggies are tender. Blend in small batches until smooth. Serve topped with croutons or parmesan cheese. Serves 4.

Cal. 98 **Fat** .4g/4% **Carb.** 19g **Fbr.** 5g **Pro.** 6g

QUICK POTATO SOUP

6 c. hot water
2 large potatoes, grated
1 carrot, grated
1/2 c. onions, chopped

1/8 t. ea. garlic powder, ground celery
    seed, onion powder, black pepper
1/2 t. salt
1 1/2 c. hot cooked brown rice

Cook all but rice over medium-high until veggies are tender. Thicken, if desired, with 1/2 c. dry milk powder and 3 T. cornstarch mixed with 1 c. warm water. Or, whisk in 1/2 c. white bean flour and cook an additional 4 minutes. Serve topped with 1/2 c. hot rice. Serves 6.

Cal. 138 **Fat** .5g/3% **Carb.** 30g **Fbr.** 3g **Pro.** 3g

BEAN CHOWDER

3 c. cooked small white beans
1 medium onion, chopped
1 lg carrot, shredded
2 ribs celery, thinly sliced

2 T. chicken-flavored bouillon
dash Worcestershire sauce
6 c. warm water
1/3 c. dry milk powder
1/2 c. white bean flour

Whisk dry milk and bean flour into 2 c. of the warm water. Combine remaining ingredients and cook until veggies are almost tender. Add milk mixture and bring to a boil, while stirring. Reduce heat to medium-low and cook an additional 2 minutes. Serves 8.

Garnish each bowl with very finely shredded carrots or fresh chopped chives.

Cal. 144 **Fat** .6g/4% **Carb.** 26g **Fbr.** 2g **Pro.** 7g

THERMOS NOODLE SOUP

1 1/2 c. dry spaghetti
2 c. boiling water
2 t. beef or vegetable bouillon

1 t. dry minced onion
1/2 t. parsley

Add all ingredients to 1 qt. thermos that has been heated with additional boiling water. Seal and tilt jar for 15 minutes. This stays warm for 24 hours in a glass or metal thermos, so it can be made in the morning for lunch or dinner. Egg noodles would hold up better during longer "cooking" times.

Cal. 238 **Fat** 1g/4% **Carb.** 48g **Fbr.** 2g **Pro.** 8g

CORN CHOWDER

2 1/2 c. hot water
1/2 c. cooked rice or cracked wheat
1/2 c. chopped onion
1/2 c. chopped celery

1 c. frozen corn
1/2 c. shredded carrots
1/2 c. frozen peas

Put all ingredients into a saucepan and bring to a boil. Lower heat to medium and cook for 5 minutes. Blend the following and add to hot mixture:

2 c. hot water
1/4 c. cornstarch mixed with
 3/4 c. dry milk powder

1 1/2 t. salt
1/8 t. pepper

Heat to just below boiling and stir until thickened. Serves 6-8.

Cal. 101 **Fat** .4g/4% **Carb.** 20g **Fbr.** 4g **Pro.** 6g

THERMOS TUNA A' LA KING

4 T. dry milk powder
2/3 c. elbow macaroni

dash salt
1 1/2 c. boiling water

Put all ingredients into a 1 qt. thermos that has been heated with additional boiling water. Stir, seal and tilt thermos for 15 minutes. Open and add:

6 1/2 oz. can tuna, undrained
1/4 t. chicken-flavored bouillon

1 t. parsley

Stir and eat. For a creamier dish, use only 1 c. boiling water and heated juice from drained tuna. Serves 2. To make without a thermos, boil water and noodles 8 minutes, then add remaining ingredients and stir lightly. Cook 2 more minutes.

Cal. 195 **Fat** .9g/4% **Carb.** 31g **Fbr.** .9g **Pro.** 15g

COMPANY DINNERS

COMPANY DINNERS are a snap when you have frozen or refrigerated cooked grains and beans ready to use. Nearly any patty or loaf recipe can be "dressed up" with a variety of special sauces.

CHINESE STEAMED BUNS

1 1/2 cups fine wheat flour
1 1/2 t. sucanat sugar
2 T. vital wheat gluten flour
1 1/2 t. regular yeast

3/4 t. salt
1 T. dry milk powder
1/4 t. dark sesame oil
1 1/4 t. canola oil
1/2 cup + 2 T. warm water

Combine all but 1/2 cup flour. Stir hard about 1 minute. Knead in enough of the remaining flour until dough is no longer sticky. Form a ball and let rest 5 minutes while mixing filling. Shape into a log about 2" across. Cut into 6 1" slices and lay each on a floured board. Pat each round to flatten and spread to about 3", being careful not to work in too much flour.

Place 1 rounded T. filling in center. Bring edges of dough up around filling, stretching a little till edges just meet; pinch to seal.

Meanwhile, over high heat, bring water for steaming to boiling. Place buns, seam side down, on lightly greased steamer racks so sides don't touch; do not let rise. (Refrigerate buns that don't fit...or allow to rise double and bake in 350°F oven for 15 minutes or until golden brown.)

Place steamer rack over boiling water. Cover steamer; steam buns 15 to 17 minutes. Makes 6 large buns.

Filling:

1 T. minced fresh green onion
1/4 cup ground gluten or dry TVP
1/2 c. shredded cabbage
1 t. sugar
1 1/2 t. cornstarch

1/8 t. minced garlic
1/4 t. grated ginger root
1 pinch 5-spice powder
1 T. soy sauce
1/8 t. flavored sesame oil

Combine all ingredients and stir well to mix.

Cal. 132 **Fat** 2g/13% **Carb.** 26g **Fbr.** 4g **Pro.** 5g

Note: Any of the Hot Pocket fillings in this book can be used in this recipe. See p. 14.

MINI WHEAT LOAVES MEXICANA

1 c. mild taco sauce	*3/4 c. oatmeal*
1 T. dried minced onion	*4 T. chopped ripe olives*
2 egg whites or 1 egg	*1 c. cooked rice or cracked wheat*
1/2 cup fat-free cottage cheese	*1/4 t. salt (opt.)*
1/2 t. each chili powder, cumin, oregano, basil	

Mix all ingredients. Measure six 1/2 c. portions into large muffin tins coated with cooking spray. Bake at 375°F for 25 minutes. If loaves stick to the pans, let sit 5 minutes before removing. Serves 6.

Note: Tomato sauce may be substituted for taco sauce if you prefer a milder flavor. If desired, top each Wheat Loaf with 1 T. grated cheddar cheese during last 5 minutes of baking.

Cal. 98 **Fat** 1.3g/11% **Carb.** 18g **Fbr.** 4g **Pro.** 5g

CRACKED WHEAT CHINESE

2 c. sliced celery	*1 lg. sliced onion*
1 sliced green pepper	*2 c. mung bean sprouts*
1 c. sliced mushrooms	*2 c. sliced Chinese Cabbage*

Simmer in 1/4 c. water or 1 T. canola oil until crispy-tender, about 5-8 min. Add:

2 T. chicken-flavored bouillon	*2 c. cooked rice or cracked wheat*
2 c. water	*1 t. ginger*
1 T. soy sauce	*Dash garlic salt*
	3 T. cornstarch in 1/4 c. cool water

Simmer 5 minutes, then add cornstarch mixture. Stir until thickened, about 1 minute. Serve over a combination of 2 cups cooked cracked wheat and 2 cups cooked brown rice. Serves 6.

Cal. 106 **Fat** .8g/7% **Carb.** 22g **Fbr.** 2g **Pro.** 4g

TUNA LOAVES

2 c. cooked rice or cracked wheat
2 6 1/2 oz. cans tuna
4 egg whites or 2 eggs
2 T. lemon juice

1 T. chopped dill pickles
1/4 c. chopped onion
1 t. chicken-flavored bouillon
1/4 t. pepper

Mix all ingredients and fill muffin tins coated with cooking spray, 3/4 full. Bake at 375°F for 15-20 minutes. Makes 12 mini-loaves. Top with grated cheese, if desired. Serves 6-8.

Cal. 98 **Fat** .7g/6% **Carb.** 15g **Fbr.** 4g **Pro.** 10g

CARROT LOAF

2 c. grated carrots
2 T. chopped onions
1 T. diced green pepper
2 t. chicken-flavored bouillon

1/2 c. chopped celery
1 c. fat-free cottage cheese
2 egg whites, beaten, or 1 egg
1 c. cooked rice or cracked wheat

Mix well and put into 8" square baking pan coated with cooking spray. Cover loosely with foil and bake at 350°F for 20-30 minutes. While baking, make sauce (below).

Sauce:

2 c. hot water
1/3 c. white bean flour
1 T. chicken-flavored bouillon

2 c. frozen peas
1 hard boiled egg

Whisk bean flour and bouillon into hot water and cook over medium heat (or microwave on high) until thick, about 1 minute. Then cook an additional 2 minutes. Add peas and egg and heat through. Spoon over hot carrot loaf.

Note: This loaf can be baked in muffin tins coated with cooking spray, 3/4 full, at 350°F for 20 minutes. Top with cheese or sauce. Serves 6.

Cal. 170 **Fat** .7g/4% **Carb.** 30g **Fbr.** 6g **Pro.** 17g

CHICKEN FLAVORED PILAF

2 c. water
3 T. chopped onion
1 c. raw rice or cracked wheat

1/8 t. pepper
2 t. chicken-flavored bouillon

Bring all ingredients to a boil in a saucepan over high heat. Cover, reduce heat and simmer for 15 minutes. Serves 4.

Cal. 121 **Fat** 1.5g/3% **Carb.** 26g **Fbr.** 7g **Pro.** 5g

Variations:

BEEF FLAVORED PILAF - Substitute beef for chicken-flavored bouillon and add 1 t. Worcestershire sauce.

PARMESAN PILAF - Increase onion to 1/4 cup. Just before serving, add 1/2 c. Parmesan cheese and sprinkle with freshly chopped parsley, chives or green onions.

PICANTE PILAF - To basic Chicken Flavored Pilaf ingredients, add 1/4 c. mild Picante Sauce (Pace's). Top individual servings with shredded cheese, if desired.

GINNI'S TORTILLA FLIPS

1 c. cooked brown rice
1/2 c. fat-free mayonnaise
1/4 c. Picante sauce or taco sauce
1 c. diced yellow onion

1 T. chopped green onion tops
1 c. fat-free cottage cheese
1 t. prepared mustard
1 T. chicken-flavored bouillon
8 flour tortillas

Heat tortilla in dry skillet over medium heat. Flip, spread with 1/2 c. mixture. Flip one side over, cover pan, and heat through. Serves 8.

Note: If desired, use grated cheddar or mozzarella cheese in place of cottage cheese.

Cal. 177 **Fat** 2.8g/14% **Carb.** 30g **Fbr.** 1g **Pro.** 8g

YEAST BREADS

Yeast breads made with 100% whole wheat flour take longer to rise than white flour breads. Since they take longer than 30 minutes from start to finish, they don't really fit into my "fast" recipe categories. However, I have found that having these breads on hand greatly increases the number of quick meals I can put together, especially with flour tortillas and pita pockets. I have included my favorite recipes for those that have time to bake, even if only occasionally.

ALL bread recipes that call for wheat flour have been tested with freshly ground whole wheat flour from hard winter wheat (as opposed to white or wheat flour purchased from a grocery store). "Wheat" Flour that is commercially ground to be sold in stores generally has the germ removed and sometimes part of the bran. The bran, or outer layer of the kernel, contains carbohydrates, proteins, vitamins, minerals — especially iron — and fiber. The germ (the part that would grow when sprouted or grown) contains a high concentration of vitamin E, B vitamins, iron and other minerals, fats, proteins, fiber and carbohydrates.

White flour makes great glue for craft projects. Whole wheat flour is rich in bran and does NOT make a good glue. This natural bran is what helps aid the body in digesting and assimilating foods, as well as moving them quickly along...too quickly if you're not used to whole grains and you eat too much at one time.

Refrigerate flours and cracked grains or beans, as they start to deteriorate if not refrigerated or frozen. Rancid foods have been proven to be carcinogenic, so do not buy or store large quantities cracked wheat or whole wheat flour unless you have refrigerator or freezer storage space.

YEAST BREADS

Sorry, these can NOT be made in 30 minutes or less, but breads are such an important part of making a quick meal that I am including my favorites here...

REDUCE RISING TIME WITH MICRO-RISE TECHNIQUE

Micro-Rise your bread dough and you'll save hours of rising time! In **"Bread in Half the Time"** by Eckhardt and Butts, the authors have perfected a method for using the microwave to cut 1st rising time from 1-2 hours down to about 10 minutes! With the aid of a food processor and a microwave, they turn out real yeast bread in only 90 minutes. Their instructions for micro-rising are very detailed to work with any type of microwave, so I'll give you a shortened version here that works for most microwaves that allow you to change power levels. It works best in ovens with a turntable. I recommend the book for those who want a real adventure in quick bread making, in addition to many quick-cooking tips.

When yeast dough (any recipe) is mixed and ready to rise, shape into a "donut" and place in a large, flat microwave dish. Cover with plastic wrap. Place in microwave along with an 8 oz. glass of cool water. In a microwave with power levels ranging from 1 to 10, set on level 3 and microwave for 3 minutes. Let rest 6 minutes. Microwave another 3 minutes, again on level 3. Dough should be warm and almost doubled.

GLUTEN-FREE BAKED GOODS

For those with wheat or gluten allergies or intolerances, this gluten-free (GF) flour mixture can be mixed in advance and used in place of wheat flour in most baked goods. Adding extra protein in the form of eggs or beaten egg whites helps produce a lighter product.

These flours can be found at your local health food store.

RITA'S GLUTEN-FREE BAKING MIX

3 c. brown rice flour   *1 1/2 c. potato starch flour*
1 c. tapioca flour   *1 c. pinto bean flour*
2/3 c. corn flour   *1/2 c. teff flour*
2 t. xanthan gum

FOCACCIA - BREAD MIXER

This popular flatbread is full of possibilities!

1 1/3 c. water
2 T. applesauce or canola oil
3 T. honey
1 t. salt

3 T. vital wheat gluten flour
3 2/3 c. whole wheat flour
1 T. active dry yeast

In mixer bowl, combine water with applesauce or canola oil, honey, and half of combined flour mixture. Mix on high for 4 minutes. Add remaining flour (and additional water if necessary), and mix until dough forms a ball that pulls away from the sides. Let rest 5 minutes. Turn onto floured board and knead 1 minute.

With your thumbs, make a hole in the center to form a donut shape and place in a mixing bowl that has been sprinkled with a little flour. Cover with plastic wrap and micro-rise (see p. 41) until doubled.

Place dough on a lightly floured board; roll and stretch into an 8" circle, about 1/2" thick. Place on baking sheet sprinkled with cornmeal and set aside to rise until puffy, about 10 minutes. Spritz with cooking spray and sprinkle with coarse salt or one of the toppings below. Just before baking, press fingertips into the dough to make deep dimples.

Bake in a preheated 400°F oven for 15-20 minutes, or until golden brown. Tear into chunks or serve in wedges.

Cal. 217 **Fat** 1.1g/4% **Carb.** 48g **Fbr.** 7g **Pro.** 8g

Toppings (to cover 2 flatbreads):

ONION

1 t. butter or olive oil
1/2 t. fresh or dried parsley

1 large yellow or white onion
black pepper to taste

Separate onions into rings and sauté in butter. Arrange on flatbread. Sprinkle with parsley and black pepper.

GARLIC-PARMESAN

1/4 c. dried parmesan cheese   1/4 t. garlic powder
1/4 t. onion powder
Combine and sprinkle on flatbread.

BLACK OLIVE (definitely NOT low-fat!)

1 c. sliced black olives   1/4 t. cumin
3/4 c. chopped tomatoes   black pepper to taste
1/2 t. chili powder   1 c. shredded cheese (opt.)
Arrange olives and tomatoes on flatbread. Sprinkle with combined spices. Top with cheese, if used.

RED PEPPER

7 oz. jar roasted peppers, drained   1/2 c. green onions, cut into 1/2" pieces
Arrange sliced peppers and onions on flatbread.

RAISIN

1 c. raisins   1/4 c. honey
1 t. cinnamon
Warm raisins mixed with honey and spoon onto flatbread. Sprinkle with cinnamon.

DATE-NUT

1 c. chopped dates   1/4 c. chopped almonds or walnuts
1/4 c. turbinado sugar or sucanat   1/8 t. nutmeg
Arrange dates and nuts on flatbread. Sprinkle with sugar and nutmeg.

APPLE-CINNAMON

3/4 c. applesauce   1/4 c. turbinado sugar or sucanat
1 apple, sliced in very thin wedges   1 t. cinnamon
Spread flatbread with applesauce. Arrange apple wedges in a pleasing pattern. Sprinkle with sugar and cinnamon.

GINNI'S APPLE-CINNAMON ROLLS

3 c. fine wheat flour
3 T. white bean flour
3 T. turbinado sugar or sucanat
3 T. gluten flour
1 t. salt

1/4 c. non-instant dry milk powder
1 1/2 t. active dry yeast
1/4 c. applesauce or canola oil
1 t. vanilla
1 1/3 c. warm water

Filling
1/2 c. unsweetened applesauce
3/4 c. turbinado sugar or sucanat

3/4 c. raisins
2 t. cinnamon

Mix dry ingredients and save out 1/2 cup. Make a nest in the flour and add applesauce or canola oil and water. Mix well for 1 minute, then add remaining flour a little at a time until dough is no longer sticky. Let rest 15 minutes. Turn onto floured board and knead 1 minute. Return to mixing bowl that has been sprinkled with a little flour.

Cover and let rise in a warm place (or micro-rise - see p. 41) until doubled. Knead 3-4 times, then flatten and roll into a 1/4" thick rectangle. Spread with applesauce, raisins (or dates), turbinado sugar and cinnamon.

Roll up like a jelly roll. Pinch edges to seal. Cut in nine slices 1 1/2" thick*. Place close together in one 9" x 13" glass baking pan coated with cooking spray. Cover with a dish towel and let rise (or micro-rise - see p. 41) in a warm place until doubled. Bake 15-20 minutes in a 375°F oven.

Cal. 281 **Fat** .9g/3% **Carb.** 65g **Fbr.** 7g **Pro.** 8g

*Cutting Tip: Slide a long piece of dental floss or heavy thread under rolled dough. Bring ends up and cross them over the dough, pulling so they meet and "pinch" the dough into round slices (sort of like tying a shoelace). This method works better than a knife, which often smashes the dough.

HOT POCKETS

3 c. whole wheat flour
1 t. salt
2 t. active dry yeast

1 1/8 c. water
2 T. applesauce or canola oil
1 T. honey

Place dry ingredients in a bowl. Make a nest and add water, applesauce or canola oil and honey. Mix well until mixture forms a smooth ball, adding additional water or flour as needed. Let rest 15 minutes. Pinch off 1/2 cup portions of dough and roll or press into a 4" circle. Place filling in center and seal edges well, using a little water along one edge. Place on baking sheet. (It doesn't seem to make much difference whether these "pockets" go through another rising process or not, so I usually bake them at this point. If you have the time, place in a warm place to rise until almost double.) Bake at 350°F for 20-30 minutes, or until golden brown.

See p. 15 for Veggie Taco, Pizza, and Fruit filling recipes.

Cal. 220 **Fat** 1.2g/5% **Carb.** 48g **Fbr.** 8g **Pro.** 9g

PARMESAN BREADSTICKS

3 c. whole wheat flour
1 t. salt
2 t. active dry yeast
1/4 c. dry Parmesan cheese

1/2 t. ea. garlic powder and oregano
2 T. applesauce or canola oil
1 T. honey
1 1/4 c. water

Place dry ingredients in a bowl. Make a nest and add applesauce or canola oil, honey and water. Mix well until mixture forms a smooth ball, adding additional water or flour as needed. Micro-rise, then roll into 9" x 13" rectangle. Place in a 9" x 13" glass pan coated with cooking spray. Cut the dough into ten 13" strips. Then, cut the strips in half so you have twenty 6 1/2" strips.

Coat the breadsticks with cooking spray and sprinkle with an additional 1/4 c. Parmesan cheese. Let rest 25 minutes in a warm place to rise double. Bake at 375°F for 15-20 minutes, or until golden brown. If desired, spray breadsticks again and add an additional 1/4 c. Parmesan and broil for 2-3 minutes until the cheese starts to turn light brown. Serve hot.

Cal. 70 **Fat** .6g/7% **Carb.** 15g **Fbr.** 2g **Pro.** 3g

SOFT PRETZELS

3 c. whole wheat flour
3/4 c. vital wheat gluten flour
2 1/2 t. active dry yeast
1 t. salt

1 1/2 c. hot water
1 T. applesauce or canola oil
1 t. honey

Place dry ingredients in a bowl. Make a nest and add remaining ingredients. Mix well until mixture forms a smooth ball, adding additional water or flour as needed. Form into a donut shape and micro-rise (see p. 41), then roll into 9" x 13" rectangle on a lightly oiled board. Cut the dough into 13 8" strips. Roll each strip into a "snake" approximately 16" long with tapered ends. Knot each into a pretzel shape. Place the pretzels on a baking sheet sprinkled with cornmeal. Place in a warm spot to rise nearly double.

Meanwhile, combine 1 qt. boiling water, 1/4 c. baking soda and 1 T. honey in a large saucepan over medium heat. When pretzels have nearly doubled, slide 3 at a time into the water bath and simmer for 30 seconds per side, turning once with a slotted spoon. Lift from the water and place on a baking sheet. Sprinkle tops with coarse salt.

Bake in a 425°F oven for 15 minutes, or until evenly browned. Serve hot.

Cal. 98 **Fat** .6g/5% **Carb.** 21g **Fbr.** 4g **Pro.** 4g

PITA POCKETS

1 1/4 c. warm water
1/4 c. buttermilk
2 c. whole wheat flour

1 T. yeast
1 t. salt

Mix well for about 3 minutes by hand, then gradually add another 1 1/2 to 2 cups flour and knead this stiff dough about 10 min. Cover and let rise about 45 minutes in a warm place (If you're in a hurry, omit this step). Place on a floured surface and shape into a long log, about 2" in diameter. Cut in 1 1/2" slices. Shape into balls and roll from center out to edges into circles about 7-9" in diameter. Place on preheated baking sheet on the lowest shelf of a 500°F oven for about 4-6 minutes, or until pita puffs all over and browns slightly. Remove from oven, cover with a towel until cool, then store in plastic bag in fridge or freezer.

Cal. 146 **Fat** .9g/5% **Carb.** 30g **Fbr.** 5g **Pro.** 7g

SUB SANDWICH ROLLS

This dough also makes excellent pizza dough.

3 1/4 c. whole wheat flour
3 T. gluten flour
1 1/2 t. active dry yeast
1 t. salt

1/2 t. turbinado sugar or sucanat
1 t. lemon juice
1 1/4 c. water

Mix dry ingredients. Make a "nest" in the flour and add lemon juice and water. Mix well for 1 minute, then add additional flour, if necessary, until dough loses its stickiness. Let rest 30 minutes. Turn onto floured board and knead 1 minute. Micro-rise (see p. 41).

Divide dough into 6 equal pieces, flatten and shape into 6 oblongs, approximately 3" wide and 1" high. Place on baking sheet coated with cooking spray and set aside to rise until double.

Preheat oven to 425°F. With a sharp knife, place 4 diagonal slashes across the top of each roll, about 1/4" deep. Bake 15 minutes, then reduce heat to 375°F and bake for an additional 10 to 15 minutes or until golden brown.

These rolls make an excellent meal when filled with shredded lettuce, Grain and Garden Burger, flavored gluten, or flavored "Cheeseburger" and topped with mustard, fat-free mayonnaise, catsup, etc.

Cal. 98 **Fat** .6g/5% **Carb.** 21g **Fbr.** 4g **Pro.** 4g

BREAD MACHINE RECIPES

There are many different automatic bread machines available today. Many of the less expensive models I tried had faulty temperature controls and either undercooked or overcooked my whole wheat and wheat-free breads, which require longer cooking at cooler temperatures. You will have the best success with those models that have a special "whole wheat bread" setting.

My favorite bread machine is the Zojirushi Home Bakery, which can be purchased from many Bosch distributors, or order from Bob's Red Mill, 1-800-553-2258.

No matter which kind you buy, you will have to adjust your recipes to your altitude and room temperature. Once you get used to the look and feel of a "perfect" batch of dough, you can adjust recipes to include a wide variety of ingredients, such as cracked grains, seeds, fruits, nuts, specialty flours, etc.

100% WHOLE WHEAT BREAD

1 1/3 c. warm water
2 T. applesauce or canola oil
3 T. sucanat or brown sugar
1 t. salt

3 2/3 c. whole wheat flour
3 T. vital wheat gluten flour
1 T. active dry yeast

Measure all ingredients except yeast into baking pan in the order listed. Make a depression in the middle of flour and sprinkle yeast into it, ensuring that the yeast does not touch any liquids. Place pan in baking unit and close lid. Select proper course and crust control setting. Bread slices best when it is allowed to cool before slicing, for those who can stand to wait that long!

**Using an electric bread mixer, combine all ingredients and knead 6 minutes. Cover and let rest 10 minutes. Knead 4 minutes. Turn dough onto lightly oiled board and shape into 2 loaves. Place in pans to rise until doubled. Bake at 350°F for 40-50 minutes, until golden brown and loaf sounds hollow when tapped.

Cal. 105 **Fat** .5g/5% **Carb.** 23g **Fbr.** 4g **Pro.** 4g

WHOLE WHEAT 'N SEED BREAD

1 1/4 c. warm water
3 T. applesauce or canola oil
3 T. honey or molasses
2 T. flax seeds, coarsely ground*
3 T. sunflower seeds, coarsely ground*

3 c. whole wheat flour
1 1/2 t. salt
3 T. + 1 t. vital gluten flour
1 T. active dry yeast

*Use a blender or seed grinder to grind seeds to a fine meal.

Measure all ingredients except yeast into baking pan in the order listed. Make a depression in the middle of flour and sprinkle yeast into it, ensuring that the yeast does not touch any liquids. Place pan in baking unit and close lid. Select proper course and crust control setting.

**Using an electric bread mixer, combine all ingredients and knead 6 minutes. Cover and let rest 10 minutes. Knead 4 minutes. Turn dough onto lightly oiled board and shape into 2 loaves. Place in pans to rise until doubled. Bake at 350°F for 40-50 minutes, until golden brown and loaf sounds hollow when tapped.

Cal. 101 **Fat** .9g/7% **Carb.** 21g **Fbr.** 3g **Pro.** 4g

QUICK BREADS

Whole grain breads, hot from the oven (or re-heated in the microwave), are perfect for snacks as well as at any meal of the day.

Most recipes in this section are made without added oils. Usually, applesauce is substituted for oil in equal quantities. However, if you cook for active adults or growing children, you can safely add oils, as directed in each recipe.

Many recipes call for bean flours that can be ground at home or purchased from many health food stores. See p. 186 for grinding instructions.

CORNMEAL TORTILLAS

1 c. boiling water	*1/4 c. fine whole wheat flour*
2 t. chicken-flavored bouillon	*3/4 c. cornmeal*
2 t. canola oil	*1 T. low-fat buttermilk*

Add bouillon and oil to boiling water, then stir in flour and cornmeal until well mixed. Mix in buttermilk. Shape into 1" balls, then place each on a floured surface and roll into 6" circles. Cook in a hot, ungreased skillet until the edges are crisp and brown. Or, cook only until firm and slightly browned, then turn over, add filling and roll. Corn tortillas are delicious served plain, buttered, or with a variety of toppings or fillings. Makes 12.

Cal. 55 **Fat** 1.1g/18% **Carb.** 10g **Fbr.** .9g **Pro.** 2g

WHEAT AND SESAME TORTILLAS

2 c. whole wheat flour	*2 T. butter or applesauce*
3 T. dry milk powder	*1/2 t. salt*
1/3 c. sesame seeds	*2 T. yogurt*
extra flour for board	*1/2 c. lukewarm water*

Combine dry ingredients. Use hand or electric beaters to cut in butter or applesauce until mixture resembles fine crumbs. Slowly pour in water and yogurt, mixing lightly with a fork. On a floured board, knead dough until smooth and elastic, about 5 minutes. Shape into a ball, cover and let stand for 10 minutes.

Divide and shape dough into 8 balls. Cover, removing one ball at a time and roll paper-thin on floured board. Place on heavy, hot, ungreased skillet, over medium-high heat. Blisters should appear right away. Brown on one side and turn. Cook about 30 seconds. Makes eight 9-inch tortillas.

Cal. 255 **Fat** 5.2g/18% **Carb.** 38g **Fbr.** 4g **Pro.** 16g

CINNAMON-RAISIN MUFFINS

1/3 c. honey
2/3 c. orange juice
1 c. raisins
3 T. lemon juice
2 ripe bananas, mashed
1/3 c. applesauce or canola oil

2 c. whole wheat flour
1 t. baking powder
1 t. baking soda
1/2 t. salt
1 1/2 t. cinnamon

In a small saucepan, bring honey, orange juice and raisins to a boil. Remove from heat and let cool while assembling other ingredients. Combine all moist ingredients. Using electric mixer, beat well. Add remaining ingredients and beat until smooth. Coat 6 muffin tins with cooking spray and fill 3/4 full. Bake at 350°F 25 minutes.

Cal. 161 **Fat** .6g/3% **Carb.** 40g **Fbr.** 4g **Pro.** 4g

BANANA SPICE MUFFINS

2 ripe bananas, mashed
1/3 c. honey
2/3 c. orange juice
3 T. lemon juice
1/3 c. applesauce or canola oil

2 c. whole wheat flour
1 t. baking powder
1 t. baking soda
1/2 t. salt
1 t. powdered allspice

Using electric mixer, beat moist ingredients. Add remaining ingredients and beat until smooth. Fill muffin tins, coated with cooking spray, 3/4 full. Bake at 350°F 25 minutes.

Cal. 125 **Fat** .5g/3% **Carb.** 30g **Fbr.** 3g **Pro.** 3g

GOLDEN OAT BRAN MUFFINS

2 c. oat bran cereal, uncooked
1/2 c. white bean flour
2 t. baking powder
2 T. buttermilk powder
   or tofu powder

1/2 t. salt (opt.)
1/2 c. raisins
1/2 c. apple juice concentrate
1 c. water
2 egg whites, beaten stiff

Combine all dry ingredients. Make a nest and stir in remaining ingredients, folding in egg whites last.

Fill muffin tins coated with baking spray 2/3 full and bake at 400° 15-20 minutes. Makes 6 lg. muffins.

Cal. 80 **Fat** .5g/5% **Carb.** 20g **Fbr.** 5g **Pro.** 4g

APPLE-CINNAMON MUFFINS

1 1/2 c. whole wheat flour
3/4 c. uncooked farina*
1 T. baking powder
1/2 t. salt
3 T. dry milk powder

1 t. cinnamon
1/2 c. honey
1 c. water
3/4 c. applesauce or canola oil
1/2 t. vanilla
2 egg whites, beaten (opt.)

Combine all dry ingredients. Make a "nest" and stir in remaining ingredients, folding in egg whites last.

Fill muffin tins coated with baking spray 2/3 full and bake at 400°F 15-20 minutes. Makes 6 large muffins.

Note: If oil is used, eliminate egg whites and add 1 egg.
*Farina is very finely cracked wheat or rice. See p. 7.

Cal. 80 **Fat** .5g/5% **Carb.** 20g **Fbr.** 5g **Pro.** 4g

CORN MUFFINS

1 c. wheat flour
1 T. baking powder
2 T. dry milk powder
3/4 c. cornmeal or corn flour
1 t. chicken bouillon

1 T. dried parsley
2 T. honey
1 c. yogurt
1/3 c. applesauce or canola oil
2 egg whites, beaten*

Mix dry ingredients, make a nest and add moist ingredients, adding egg whites last. Stir just until mixed. Fill muffin tins coated with cooking spray, 2/3 full. Bake 20-25 minutes at 325°F. These are best served hot with honey or jam. Makes 8 large muffins.

*Note: If oil is added, use only 1 egg white, unbeaten.

Cal. 133 **Fat** 1.2g/7% **Carb.** 30g **Fbr.** 9g **Pro.** 5g

REFRIGERATOR BRAN MUFFINS

6 c. flaked bran
6 c. boiling water
2 c. honey
3/4 c. applesauce or canola oil
5 egg whites, beaten*
2 T. vanilla
1/2 c. yogurt

6 c. whole wheat flour
4 T. baking powder
1 1/2 t. salt
1 1/2 c. dry milk powder
1 c. raisins
1 1/2 c. grated apples
1 T. cinnamon

Pour boiling water over bran. Let rest 10 minutes. Add honey, oil, vanilla and egg whites. Stir well. Add remaining ingredients and mix well. Fill muffin tins coated with cooking spray, 2/3 full and bake at 400°F 15-20 minutes. Because of the yogurt, this mixture stores well for several weeks in the refrigerator.

*Note: If oil is added, eliminate egg whites and add 2 eggs, unbeaten.

Cal. 97 **Fat** .4g/4% **Carb.** 24g **Fbr.** 4g **Pro.** 3g

BUTTERMILK OATMEAL MUFFINS

1 c. rolled oats
1 c. buttermilk
2 egg whites, beaten*
1/4 c. warmed honey
1/3 c. applesauce

1/3 c. oil, opt.
1 t. baking soda
1/2 t. salt
1 c. whole wheat flour

Soak oats in buttermilk for at least 1/2 hour. Preheat oven to 425°F. Fold beaten egg white into oat mixture, then add remaining ingredients, stirring only until ingredients are combined. Bake in muffin tins coated with cooking spray for 15 to 20 minutes, or until browned. Makes 12 muffins.

*Note: If oil is added, use only 1 egg white (or 1 egg), unbeaten.

Cal. 92 **Fat** .7g/6% **Carb.** 19g **Fbr.** 2g **Pro.** 4g

DATE-NUT MUFFINS

2 T. dry milk powder
1 c. whole wheat flour
1/4 t. salt
1 T. baking powder
1 c. chopped nuts or oatmeal
1/2 c. chopped dates

3/4 c. cooked cracked wheat
1/2 c. buttermilk
1/4 c. oil, opt.
1/3 c. honey
1 t. vanilla
1/4 c. applesauce
2 egg whites, beaten*

Measure dry ingredients into a mixing bowl. Make a "nest" and add liquid ingredients to center of bowl, adding egg whites last. Stir just enough to moisten. Fill muffin tins coated with cooking spray, 3/4 full and bake in 400°F oven 20-25 minutes. Makes 12 muffins.

*Note: If oil is added, use only 1 egg white or 1 egg, unbeaten.

Cal. 143 **Fat** .4g/2% **Carb.** 30g **Fbr.** 2g **Pro.** 7g

WHOLE WHEAT CREPES

1/2 c. whole wheat flour
1/2 c. water
1/4 t. salt (opt.)

1 T. oil (opt.)
1 T. dry milk powder
3 egg whites or 2 eggs

Put all in blender and mix just until smooth. Pour scant 1/4 cup batter on lightly greased hot skillet. Lift and tilt skillet to spread batter. Cook on medium heat. Batter dulls when cooked on 1 side. Flip and cook on other side.

Cover and place in warm oven while others cook. Excellent filled with scrambled eggs made with onions, green pepper and a little Picante sauce. Makes 12 crepes.

To freeze, put waxed paper or plastic wrap between each 4-5 cooked crepes. Wrap securely in plastic wrap, or place in plastic container. Use within 2 months.

Cal. 28 **Fat** .5g/15% **Carb.** 4g **Fbr.** .6g **Pro.** 2g

WHOLE WHEAT FLOUR TORTILLAS

2 c. fine whole wheat flour
1 1/4 t. baking powder
3/4 c. water

1/2 t. salt
1 T. canola oil

Mix all together in a 2-qt. bowl. Knead about 5 minutes, until elastic. Let rest 15 minutes, then cut dough into 10 equal portions.

Roll each into a ball, then roll out on floured surface until very thin and round. Brown on both sides in an ungreased skillet over medium-high heat. Makes 10 tortillas.

Cal. 78 **Fat** 1.5g/16% **Carb.** 15g **Fbr.** 2g **Pro.** 3g

LOW-FAT WHEATQUICK

8 1/3 c. whole wheat flour   1/3 c. baking powder
1 T. salt   1 1/3 c. dry milk powder
2 t. baking soda

Mix well, using electric mixer or hand beater. Refrigerate in covered container and use as needed. Use within 3 months. Makes 10 cups.
*If you use whole eggs and oil in baking, you may make the following adjustments to this recipe: If a recipe calls for 2 beaten egg whites, you may use 1 whole egg, unbeaten. In place of 3 egg whites, use 2 eggs. Add 1 c. oil to this recipe and omit applesauce or oil from the following recipes:

HONEY-NUT MUFFINS

2 c. WheatQuick   3/4 c. water
1/4 c. honey or brown sugar   2 egg whites, beaten
1 c. chopped nuts or oatmeal   3 T. applesauce or canola oil

Mix just until evenly moistened, then fold in egg whites. Fill 10 paper-lined muffin cups to the top. Bake 15 minutes at 400°F.

Cal. 121 **Fat** .9g/6% **Carb.** 25g **Fbr.** 3g **Pro.** 5g each

For Cinnamuffins, add 1 t. cinnamon and an extra 1 T. honey.

GINGERBREAD BREAKFAST MUFFINS

2 c. WheatQuick   2 T. molasses
1 t. cinnamon   1/3 c. honey
1 t. ginger   3 egg whites, beaten
3/4 c. butter milk   3 T. applesauce or canola oil

Add moist ingredients to dry ones and mix lightly, folding in egg whites last. Fill 10 muffin cups coated with cooking spray. Bake 15 minutes at 400°F.

Cal. 116 **Fat** .4g/3% **Carb.** 24g **Fbr.** 3g **Pro.** 4g each

PINEAPPLE STICKY BUNS

1/2 c. applesauce or canola oil　　*1/2 c. drained crushed pineapple*
1 t. cinnamon　　*1/2 c. brown sugar or honey*

Mix and divide into 12 muffin cups coated with cooking spray. Top with batter:
2 c. WheatQuick　　*1/3 c. honey or brown sugar*
3/4 c. pineapple juice　　*3 egg whites, beaten*
(drained from crushed pineapple)

Mix batter lightly and spoon over pineapple mixture. Bake 15 to 20 minutes at 400°F. Invert on tray or rack immediately to prevent sticking.

Cal. 180 **Fat** .4g/2% **Carb.** 44g **Fbr.** 2g **Pro.** 4g each

PINEAPPLE NUT MUFFINS

2 c. WheatQuick　　*3 T. applesauce or canola oil*
1 c. sunflower seeds (opt.)　　*3/4 c. pineapple juice*
1 c. oatmeal or chopped nuts　　*2/3 c. raisins*
1/4 c. honey or brown sugar　　*3 egg whites, beaten*

Mix batter lightly and fill 12 muffin cups coated with cooking spray. Bake at 400°F 12-15 minutes.

Cal. 148 **Fat** .8g/5% **Carb.** 32g **Fbr.** 3g **Pro.** 5g each

WHEATQUICK PANCAKES

2 T. honey　　*1 c. buttermilk*
2 2/3 c. WheatQuick　　*1 c. water*
3 T. applesauce or canola oil　　*2 egg whites, beaten*

Beat egg whites until stiff. Mix in order given. Bake on hot griddle coated with cooking spray. Serves 4.

Cal. 321 **Fat** 1.6g/4% **Carb.** 66g **Fbr.** 8g **Pro.** 15g per serving

SNACKS

SNACK TIME, *our favorite time, can be as nutritious as regular meal time. Some snacks can be a whole meal by themselves. High-fiber whole grains and legumes are the basic ingredient in many of these snacks.*

5-MINUTE 3-BEAN DIP

1/4 cup ea. black bean flour,
  pinto bean flour,
  kidney bean flour
1/4 t. cumin

1/2 t. chili powder
2 1/2 c. warm water
3/4 t. salt (opt)
1/2 c. picante sauce

Whisk dry ingredients into warm water in a medium saucepan and bring to a boil over medium-high heat. Stir until mixture boils, then reduce heat and cover pan. Cook an additional 4 minutes, stirring once. Remove from heat. Add Picante sauce. Serve hot or cold. This recipe makes great burrito filling!

Cal. 54 **Fat** .2g/4% **Carb.** 10g **Fbr.** 4g **Pro.** 3g

PINTO BEAN DIP

1/2 med. onion, minced
1/2 t. cumin
1 T. beef-flavored bouillon
1/2 t. chili powder

1/2 t. garlic powder
1/2 t. salt
1/4 c. Picante sauce
3 c. cooked mashed pinto beans

Mix and heat through. Add 1 c. grated cheese, if desired. Serve hot in chip-lined bowls and top with chopped tomatoes and green onions. Serves 6.

Cal. 170 **Fat** .7g/4% **Carb.** 30g **Fbr.** 6g **Pro.** 17g

CRISPY PITA STRIPS

Cut the edges of each pita pocket to make 2 circles. Sprinkle the rough side with parmesan cheese and a little garlic powder. Bake in 450°F oven until slightly browned and crispy. Serve hot or cold.

Cal. 45 **Fat** .4g/8% **Carb.** 9g **Fbr.** .2g **Pro.** 2g

E-Z POTATO ROUNDS - Fat FREE!

6 medium potatoes
Parmesan cheese (opt.)

Salt and pepper

Scrub potatoes and cut out any bad spots. Cut into 1/4" slices and place rounds on baking sheet coated with cooking spray. Sprinkle generously with salt, pepper, and parmesan and bake in preheated 400°F oven for 20 minutes. Turn over, sprinkle again with seasonings and cook another 10 minutes. Cool on tray.

Cal. 110 **Fat** 0g/0% **Carb.** 26g **Fbr.** 3g **Pro.** 3g each

SKINNY FRIES - Fat FREE!

These take a while to cook, but are well worth the wait! Serve with burgers or eat them plain.

2 t. chicken-flavored bouillon	*2 egg whites or 1 egg, beaten*
2 t. pinto bean flour	*3 medium potatoes, cut in wedges*
1 1/2 T. water	*Salt and pepper*
	Parmesan cheese (opt.)

In a medium bowl, mix bouillon, flour, water and egg whites. Add potatoes and stir to coat. Place wedges on baking sheet coated with cooking spray. Sprinkle generously with salt and pepper and bake in preheated 400°F oven for 20 minutes. Turn over and cook another 10 minutes. Broil about 1 minute to brown.

Cal. 120 **Fat** 0g/0% **Carb.** 26g **Fbr.** 3g **Pro.** 4g each

"POPPED WHEAT" and seeds are an excellent source of fiber and nutrition. Since heating destroys valuable nutrients, try mixing 2/3 cooked with 1/3 uncooked seeds. (Uncooked grains would be too hard to chew.) These can be made ahead and stored for several weeks, or refrigerated and stored for months. Nuts, corn nuts, chinese noodles, mints, and carob chips can be added for an extra special touch. Note: If chewing popped wheat is a problem, substitute brown rice which is softer and easier to chew. Some brands of instant brown rice work well.

POPPED WHEAT AND SEEDS - BASIC MIX

1 c. wheat	*1 c. sunflower seeds*
1 c. brown rice	*1 c. pumpkin seeds*
1/4 c. sesame seeds	

Dry "pop" seeds and grains, one type at a time, in a heavy skillet. Mix all together. This mixture is good without salt or seasonings, but if desired, use one of the following recipes:

Cal. 86 **Fat** 4.6g/45% **Carb.** 9g **Fbr.** 2g **Pro.** 3g

B-B-Q SEED MIX

1 c. Basic Mix
1/2 t. beef-flavored bouillon

2 t. B-B-Q seasoning (powdered)

Combine all ingredients, then spray seeds and grains with enough cooking spray to make seasonings stick.

Cal. 86 **Fat** 4.8g/46% **Carb.** 9g **Fbr.** 2g **Pro.** 3g

CHINESE SEED MIX

1 c. Basic Mix
1/3 t. ginger
1 c. chinese noodles

1 t. chicken-flavored bouillon
1 T. soy sauce
1 c. freeze dried peas (optional)

Mix and heat in skillet 1-2 minutes to dry out mixture. Serve hot or cold.

Cal. 111 **Fat** 4.7g/32% **Carb.** 14g **Fbr.** 3g **Pro.** 5g

SPICED SUNFLOWER SEEDS

2 c. sunflower seeds
1 T. tamari (soy sauce)

1/2 t. chili powder

In heavy skillet, cook sunflower seeds over medium heat, stirring constantly, until they are lightly browned. Turn off heat, add soy sauce and chili powder. Stir well, reheat until dried out, then allow to cool. Pumpkin seeds, almonds or peanuts may be substituted for sunflower seeds. Or, use a combination of several kinds of nuts and seeds.

Cal. 207 **Fat** 18g/72% **Carb.** 7g **Fbr.** 4g **Pro.** 8g

CRISPY WHOLE WHEAT CRACKERS

To make crispy crackers, dough must be rolled very thin, and only enough flour added for easy handling of the dough. When overmixed, the gluten develops, and the crackers are VERY tough.

7/8 c. wheat flour	*1/2 c. water*
1 t. chicken-flavored bouillon	*1/3 c. sesame seeds*
1/4 t. ginger	*1 t. soy sauce*

Mix all together, adding more flour, if necessary, to keep the dough from being sticky. Stir only until dough holds together. Place dough on a baking sheet coated with cooking spray (one without sides works best). Roll dough out 1/8" thick. Sprinkle with salt or vegetable powder, if desired. Score with a sharp knife or pizza cutter into 1" or 2" rectangles, and bake at 350°F until lightly browned, about 15 minutes. If the edges brown too fast, take outer crackers off and continue baking. Note: For soup crackers, score in 1/2" squares and break apart when cool. Makes 1 medium tray.

Cal. 103 **Fat** .6g/5% **Carb.** 22g **Fbr.** 4g **Pro.** 4g

SMOOTHIES

Smoothies are cooling and OH so satisfying when it's hot outside (or even when it's FREEZING outside, if you wrap up in a blanket and sit by a heater!). All you need is fresh fruit, fruit juice concentrates, ice, and a good strong blender to enjoy a smoothie for a snack, or even dessert.

With the addition of sesame or sunflower seeds (blended with the liquid until smooth before adding remaining ingredients), you can create a drink high in calcium and protein, full-of-fiber and VERY filling...great for growing, active children! Best of all, smoothies are very versatile because you can vary the recipe and use any fruit available, even canned or bottled fruit.

The drinks I have added here are made with milk substitutes. To use dry milk powder, add 1/3 c. to each Smoothie recipe and substitute water for the liquid.

Growing up in Oregon, I learned to love all kinds of berries. They are readily available in the frozen food section of your grocery store. Here are some of our favorite BERRY delicious drinks to cool you off on a hot afternoon.

RED RASPBERRY SMOOTHIE

2 c. Rice Dream or milk substitute   1 t. vanilla
1 c. frozen raspberries   1/2 c. frozen apple juice concentrate
1 banana   10 ice cubes
   1 T. almonds (opt.)

Place all ingredients in blender and process on high for 2 minutes, until smooth.

Cal. 205 **Fat** .3g/1% **Carb.** 46g **Fbr.** 2g **Pro.** 1g

BLACKBERRY DELIGHT

2 c. Rice Dream or milk substitute   1 t. vanilla
1 c. frozen blackberries   1/2 c. frozen apple juice concentrate
1 banana   10 ice cubes
   1 T. raw sunflower seeds (opt.)

Place all ingredients in blender and process on high for 2 minutes, until smooth.

Cal. 235 **Fat** .4g/2% **Carb.** 54g **Fbr.** 3g **Pro.** 1g

CREAMY STRAWBERRY SMOOTHIE

2 c. Fat-Free Mocha Mix (liquid non-dairy creamer)
1 c. frozen strawberries   1 c. frozen apple juice concentrate
1 frozen banana   1 t. vanilla
   1 T. sesame seeds (opt.)

Place all ingredients in blender and process on high for 2 minutes, until smooth.

Cal. 155 **Fat** .5g/3% **Carb.** 38g **Fbr.** 2g **Pro.** 1g

BERRY BLUEBERRY MALT

2 c. Fat-Free Mocha Mix (liquid non-dairy creamer)
1 1/4 c. frozen blueberries   1 c. frozen apple juice concentrate
1 frozen banana   1 1/2 t. vanilla
2 T. malted milk powder   6 almonds (opt.)

Place all ingredients in blender and process on high for 2 minutes, until smooth.

Cal. 213 **Fat** 1.3g/5% **Carb.** 50g **Fbr.** 2g **Pro.** 2g

For more great drinks, see p. 140 in the Powdered Milk Section.

DESSERTS AND CANDIES

Most cookbooks have an overabundance of dessert recipes, usually filled with too much added fat and sugar. Naturally, those desserts will be more appealing than ones that are actually GOOD for you. However, it IS possible to enjoy desserts made with nutritious ingredients, with little or no added fat.

The whole nuts and seeds in this section add fat to a recipe, but that fat is more readily burned than fats from oils and dairy products.

In an effort to provide nutritious low-fat recipes, I have substituted oats for the nuts and seeds, or listed them as optional. In place of butter and oil, I have used applesauce.

If you have growing children or live an active life style and can handle more fats, feel free to add the nuts, seeds and oils, as listed in these recipes.

SWEDISH APPLE CAKE

1 cup whole wheat flour	*1 t. vanilla*
1 t. cinnamon	*3/4 c. honey*
1 t. baking powder	*4 egg whites*
1 t. baking soda	*2 c. apple (2 medium) chopped fine*
2 T. oatmeal	*1/2 t. vinegar*

Mix all except apple and vinegar in a bowl. This will give you a heavy, wet dough. Mix in remaining ingredients. If desired, add 3 T. canola oil or butter and use only 2 egg whites. Put in 8" square pan coated with cooking spray. Cook in 350°F oven for 35 minutes until lightly browned. Excellent served in a bowl with milk.

Cal. 174 **Fat** .4g/2% **Carb.** 42g **Fbr.** 3g **Pro.** 4g

GRAHAM CRACKERS

2 c. wheat flour	*1/4 t. soda*
scant t. baking powder	*pinch of salt*
1/3 c. dry milk powder	*1/2 t. cinnamon*

Mix in bowl. Make a nest and add:

1/3 c. applesauce or canola oil	*1 T. vanilla*
1/2 c. warm honey	*2 T. water*
1 t. vinegar or lemon juice	

As you mix, this should form a stiff pie-crust type dough. As wheat flours differ in moisture content, you may need to add more or less flour. You can add up to 1/4 c. more flour if dough is too limp.

Roll out evenly on baking sheet coated with cooking spray. Dough should be 1/8" to 1/4" thick on a large tray. Score into small or large squares, or cut shapes with cookie cutters. If you make large squares, prick with fork to allow hot air to escape. Bake at 350°F for 8-10 minutes, or until golden brown. You may need to take off the crackers around the edges at about 5-6 minutes, and then let the rest brown. These make great ice cream sandwiches or pie crust crumbs. Makes 1 large tray.

Cal. 183 **Fat** .6g/3% **Carb.** 42g **Fbr.** 4g **Pro.** 5g

BISCOTTI is a very popular version of an old-fashioned favorite - dried sweet bread. This was an excellent treat that could be easily stored, and very portable. It can be made fat-free, but unfortunately, most commercial varieties packaged for the Gift Market are loaded with extra fats and sugars. I think you'll like the results of all of the following recipes. With the addition of bean flours for a complete protein, they make a healthy snack or dessert.

ORANGE-ALMOND BISCOTTI
Makes 2 flat loaves

2 cups whole wheat flour
1 1/2 T. white bean flour
1/4 t. salt
1 cup turbinado sugar
1 T. baking powder

2 large eggs, beaten (or 4 egg whites)
1 t. vanilla extract
1/3 t. almond extract
3/4 cup whole almonds (opt.)
3 T. minced orange zest
1/3 c. water

Preheat oven to 350°F and place rack in middle position. Toast almonds, if used, and chop fine. Mix all ingredients in order given, just until combined.

Place dough on a lightly floured surface and shape into two logs, about 13"x2". Set them at least 3" apart on a baking sheet coated with cooking spray.

Bake, turning pan once, until loaves are golden and just beginning to crack on top, about 25-30 minutes. When cooled, cut each log diagonally into 20 slices. Lay the slices on the cookie sheet, cut side up, and return them to the oven.

Bake at 325°F, turning slices over half way through baking, until crisp and golden brown on both sides, about 15 minutes.

Variation: Add 1/2 cup chopped dates or soaked chopped raisins to dough.

Cal. 43 **Fat** .1g/2% **Carb.** 10g **Fbr.** 1g **Pro.** 1g per slice

Variations (Follow mixing and baking instructions on previous page):

LEMON BISCOTTI

2 cups whole wheat flour
1 1/2 T. white bean flour
1/4 t. salt
1 cup turbinado sugar
1 T. baking powder

2 large eggs, beaten (or 4 egg whites)
1 t. vanilla extract
1/3 t. lemon extract
3 T. minced zest from 1 lemon
1/3 c. water

Cal. 43 **Fat** .1g/2% **Carb.** 10g **Fbr.** 1g **Pro.** 1g per slice

HONEY BISCOTTI

2 1/4 cups whole wheat flour
1 1/2 T. white bean flour
1/4 t. salt
2/3 cup turbinado or date sugar
1 T. baking powder

2 large eggs, beaten (or 4 egg whites)
1 t. vanilla extract
3 T. honey
3 T. minced zest from 1 lemon
1/3 c. water

If desired, add 1/2 cup unhulled sesame seeds or poppy seeds to dry ingredients. Brush top of loaves with a glaze (egg white) and sprinkle with additional seeds.

Cal. 44 **Fat** .1g/3% **Carb.** 10g **Fbr.** 1g **Pro.** 1g per slice

SPICED APPLE BISCOTTI

2 1/4 c. whole wheat flour
1 1/2 T. white bean flour
1/4 t. salt
1 c. turbinado, date sugar or honey*
2 t. baking powder
1 t. baking soda
1 T. minced zest from 1 orange

2 large eggs, beaten (or 4 egg whites)
1 t. vanilla extract
1/3 t. lemon extract
1/2 t. ground cloves
1/2 t. ground cinnamon
1/4 t. ground ginger
1/3 c. apple juice concentrate
3 T. grated apple

*If using honey, increase wheat flour to 2 3/4 c.
Cal. 48 **Fat** .1g/3% **Carb.** 11g **Fbr.** 1g **Pro.** 1g per slice

CREAMY CAROB BAVARIAN

1 T. gelatin
2 T. cold water
1/4 t. mint extract
2 1/2 T. carob powder
1 c. cooked rice or cracked wheat

1/3 c. dry milk powder
1 t. vanilla
1 1/2 c. water
2/3 c. honey or sugar
1 c. minced almonds, opt.

Mix gelatin and water in a 1 quart saucepan. Blend remaining ingredients except nuts for 2 minutes on high speed. Pour into gelatin mixture, add nuts and cook over medium high heat, stirring constantly, for 4-5 minutes until mixture is thick. Pour into mold or custard cups coated with cooking spray and chill until firm. If desired, fold in 2 c. whipping cream or other non-dairy whipped topping. Note: This would also be an excellent pie filling. Serves 6.

SIMPLE CANDIES are very easy to make. Very few of us NEED sweet treats, but desserts and snacks do have a way of working themselves into our diets. My experience has been that if I have nutritious snacks available, my family enjoys better health and is less likely to want commercially manufactured goodies.

Cal. 165 **Fat** .3g/1% **Carb.** 40g **Fbr.** 4g **Pro.** 3g

PEANUT BUTTER HAYSTACKS

1/2 c. dry milk powder
1/2 c. chunky peanut butter
1/3 c. whole wheat flour

1/2 c. honey
1 t. vanilla
1 1/2 c. granola or rolled oats
1 c. shredded coconut, toasted

Cook honey to firm ball stage (245°F). Combine all but granola and coconut and knead by hand until smooth. Mix in granola and drop by spoonfuls into coconut. Roll to coat, then place on waxed paper to cool. If desired, add 1/2 c. 2-day wheat sprouts to coconut.

Note: Do not use instant milk in this recipe as the crystals do not dissolve well. Makes 3 dozen haystacks.

Cal. 152 **Fat** 6g/34% **Carb.** 21g **Fbr.** 1g **Pro.** 5g

NO-COOK PEANUT BUTTER SQUARES

3/4 c. warm melted honey　　*1 c. crunchy peanut butter*
1 t. vanilla　　*1 c. dry milk powder*

Mix well. Press into 8" square pan and cool. Cut into 1" squares (or you could roll into balls). Serve plain or decorate with a carob chip, or roll in toasted coconut, popped wheat or rice krispies. You could also add 1/4 c. carob powder along with the powdered milk to make Creamy Peanut Butter Fudge. Makes 64 squares.

Cal. 212 **Fat** 11g/43% **Carb.** 25g **Fbr.** 2g **Pro.** 7g per square

ALMOND POWER BARS
Great for Backpacking!

1 c. almonds　　*3 T. sesame seeds*
3/4 c. dates, chopped　　*3 T. sunflower seeds, toasted*
1 c. dry milk powder　　*1/2 c. warm honey*
　　1/2 c. shredded coconut

Using a hand meat grinder, food processor or strong blender, coarsely grind almonds and dates. Mix in remaining ingredients. Press into 8" square pan. Cut into 1" squares (or you could roll into balls).

Cal. 159 **Fat** 9.8g/52% **Carb.** 15g **Fbr.** 3g **Pro.** 6g per square

COCONUT MACAROONS

3/4 c. honey　　*1 c. dry milk powder*
1/4 t. almond flavoring　　*1 c. fine coconut*

Warm honey so it is fairly liquid and mix with flavoring. Add powdered milk and mix well, then add a little coconut at a time and mix in until you have a very stiff dough. Form into balls and flatten slightly. Place on baking sheet coated with cooking spray. Put pan 10" under broiler and broil about 3 minutes or until golden brown. Watch closely because they burn easily.

Cal. 108 **Fat** 2.3g/18% **Carb.** 21g **Fbr.** .6g **Pro.** 2g per macaroon

WHEAT GERM SQUARES

4 eggs or 8 egg whites
1 c. honey
2 T. carob powder
1 T. butter or applesauce

2 1/2 c. wheat germ
1 c. rolled oats or chopped nuts
1/2 t. salt
2 t. vanilla

Preheat oven to 375°F. Beat eggs until very stiff. Gradually beat in honey and butter. Stir in remaining ingredients. Pour into 9"x13" pan coated with cooking spray. Bake 25 minutes, or until center is done.

Cool in pan and cut into 2" squares.

Cal. 38 **Fat** .6g/14% **Carb.** 7g **Fbr.** 1g **Pro.** 2g per square

PINEAPPLE BARS

2 T. applesauce or canola oil
1 lg. egg white
6 oz. frozen pineapple juice conc.
1 t. vanilla
1/4 c. honey
1 c. drained pineapple chunks

1/4 c. chopped dates
1 t. baking powder
1/2 t. baking soda
1 1/8 c. whole wheat flour
1/3 c. rolled oats or chopped nuts

Beat egg white until stiff. Beat in remaining moist ingredients. Add remaining ingredients and mix well. Bake 25 minutes at 350°F in a 9"x13" pan coated with cooking spray. Cut into 48 bars 1"x1 1/2".

Cal. 31 **Fat** .1g/3% **Carb.** 7g **Fbr.** 1g **Pro.** 1g per bar

HONEY-OAT BARS

6 egg whites or 3 eggs, beaten stiff
1 c. honey
1 t. vanilla
1/4 c. applesauce or canola oil
1 1/2 c. chopped dates

1/4 t. salt
1 t. baking powder
1 1/3 c. whole wheat flour
3/4 c. rolled oats or chopped nuts

Beat eggs until stiff. Beat in honey, vanilla, applesauce or canola oil and dates. Add remaining dry ingredients and mix well. Pour into 9"x13" pan coated with cooking spray. Bake at 350°F for 25 minutes. Cool in pan. Cut in 1"x1 1/2" bars. Roll in powdered turbinado sugar, if desired. Makes 40 bars.

Cal. 67 **Fat** .2g/3% **Carb.** 16g **Fbr.** 1g **Pro.** 2g per bar

RAISIN BARS

3 eggs or 6 egg whites
1 c. honey
1 t. grated lemon rind
1/4 t. salt

1 t. baking powder
1 c. whole wheat flour
1/2 c. raisins
1/2 c. rolled oats or chopped nuts
1/4 c. applesauce or canola oil

Beat eggs until stiff. Gradually beat in honey. Mix in remaining ingredients. Spread in 9"x13" pan coated with cooking spray. Bake 25 minutes at 325°F for 25 minutes. Cool in pan. Cut in 1" x 1 1/2" bars. Makes 40 bars.

Cal. 49 **Fat** .1g/2% **Carb.** 12g **Fbr.** 1g **Pro.** 1g per bar

BETHLEHEM DATE BARS

This is our favorite Christmas Bar. We love dates and eat them often at Christmas, knowing they were used in Bethlehem at the time of Christ's birth.

3 eggs
1 c. turbinado sugar or honey
1/4 c. applesauce, butter,
    or canola oil
2 c. chopped dates
1 c. chopped nuts
1 c. find wheat flour

1 t. baking powder
1/8 t. salt
1/4 t. powdered cloves
1/4 t. powdered cinnamon
1 t. vanilla
powdered sugar (optional)

Start oven set at 325°F. Coat a 9" x 13" pan with cooking spray. Beat eggs and applesauce, butter, or oil until light. Gradually add the sugar or honey and beat until smooth. Stir in the remaining ingredients, except powdered sugar, and mix well.

Spread mixture in the pan. Bake about 25 minutes. Let cool. Cut in strips or bars and roll each in powdered sugar. Makes 36 bars.

Cal. 101 **Fat** 3.9g/32% **Carb.** 16g **Fbr.** 2g **Pro.** 2g per square

DATE-NUT PUDDING

This Christmas Pudding has been a favorite in our family for generations.

2 c. dates, chopped fine
1 t. baking soda
1 c. boiling water
***
2 T. applesauce or butter

1 c. honey
1 egg
1 t. baking powder
1/2 c. chopped nuts
1/2 t. salt
2 3/4 c. whole wheat flour

Add dates and soda to boiling water. Let stand until cool. Cream applesauce or butter, honey and egg. Add dry ingredients and mix well. Add date mixture and beat thoroughly. Fill clean, washed 10 3/4 oz. soup cans (labels removed) 1/2 full. Place cans in a large pan filled with boiling water. Cover with a lid or foil and steam for 1 hour, or until center of each pudding is firm. Allow to cool slightly, then loosen puddings with a knife and slide out. Cut into 2" slices and serve warm, topped with milk or Date-Nut Pudding Sauce. Serves 12.

Cal. 278 **Fat** 2g/6% **Carb.** 56g **Fbr.** 5g **Pro.** 6g per serving

DATE-NUT PUDDING SAUCE

1 T. butter
1 t. vanilla
2 T. cornstarch

1 c. honey
1 c. hot water
juice of 1/2 lemon

In a small saucepan, melt butter. Add sugar mixed with cornstarch. Add remaining ingredients and stir until done.

Cal. 100 **Fat** .9g/8% **Carb.** 25g **Fbr.** 0g **Pro.** 0g per serving

Sprouting

Welcome to the wonderful world of sprouting... the BEST way to get the FRESHEST foods on earth!

It is my hope that you will enjoy experimenting with the recipes in this section and that you will find many sprouts and sprout recipes your family will love!

SPROUTS

"Sprouts grow practically anywhere; flourish in any climate, during any season of the year; need neither soil nor sunshine; are ready for harvest in 2-5 days; taste delicious raw or cooked; have no waste; and are so nutritious that they are one of the most complete foods known to man, rivaling meat in protein and citrus fruits in vitamin C at a fraction of the cost." (Northrup King Co., Consumer Products Division)

Growing a "garden" of sprouts requires much less effort than traditional outdoor or window gardens. Rinsing and draining several different kinds of sprouts takes only about 15 minutes a day and can provide a large variety of fresh vegetables not available in markets...and all for just pennies a day.

SPROUTING ADDS ENZYMES

Sprouting changes the composition of dried beans and legumes so that they can be easily digested with little or no cooking. The "gas" or flatulence many people experience when eating beans is caused by the indigestible carbohydrates which are changed into digestible carbohydrates during the sprouting process.

Sprouting also adds enzymes that convert starches to sugars and break down proteins into individual amino acids so our bodies do not have to work so hard to process the foods we eat.

SPROUTS ARE VALUABLE SOURCES
OF VITAMINS, MINERALS AND PROTEINS

Sprouted grains and beans (legumes) increase in vitamins A, B and C, E, and K. Riboflavin and folic acid increase up to 13 times the original amount present in dry seeds. Two of the most important amino acids necessary for the body to manufacture proteins are lysine and tryptophan, which are increased significantly during sprouting. Vitamin C increases up to 600% in some cases. (Great Tasting Health Foods, by Robert Rodale.)

Leafy, green sprouts such as alfalfa, buckwheat lettuce and wheat grass, contain a rich supply of chlorophyll, a valuable source of vitamin A and protein. Research conducted by Dr. Charles R. Shaw, M.D., professor of biology at the University of Texas System Cancer Center in Houston, indicates the possibility that chlorophyll prevents formation of carcinoma (cancer) in mice."The chlorophyll appears to exert its inhibitory effect (up to 99 percent effective!!) by interfering with enzymes which activate the carcinogens." (This information applies to uncooked sprouts.)

Nutrients and volume increase during sprouting, but calories do not, making sprouts a good low calorie addition to any meal, or even as a meal by themselves. Many people use a variety of sauces and dressings added to a generous serving of various sprouts for a super delicious, nutritious, sprout meal or snack. Children love to eat cool, crisp, clover and alfalfa sprouts by the handful. It is best to serve a wide variety of sprouts to insure a balanced diet, since no one type of sprout contains all the essential nutrients to maintain good health.

HEATING DESTROYS NUTRIENTS

Heating destroys some of the vitamin C in ALL foods. The most significant loss (60%) occurs when foods are boiled in water that is then discarded. Steamed or stir-fried foods lose only 20-30% of their vitamin C content.

All enzymes are destroyed at temperatures over 130°F, so most of the enzymes added by sprouting will be lost if foods are cooked at high temperatures for more than 2-3 minutes. However, most people don't get too excited about eating ALL their food raw, and many sprouted beans just don't taste good when eaten raw. The easiest way to ensure a sufficient supply of nutrients when sprouts must be cooked is to serve a generous helping of raw sprouts at the same meal in salads, sandwiches, dips, drinks or as snacks.

SPROUTED BEANS ARE MORE "FRIENDLY"

Cooking sprouted beans at high temperatures destroys all enzymes, but the conversion of starches to sugars that occurs during sprouting still allows cooked beans to be digested easily. (Adding meat, or any animal product, to sprouted beans will still cause some gas to be produced.) White beans (Small White, Navy, Lima, Soy, etc), peas and lentils are less likely to produce gas and can often be substituted for pinto or red beans.

SPROUTS AS PROTEIN FOODS

Amino acids are the building blocks our body uses to manufacture proteins. Good quality protein foods contain sufficient quantities of the eight amino acids considered "essential," meaning they cannot be manufactured by the body. Eating foods that contain those eight amino acids supplies our bodies with the building blocks necessary to do the work of combining for us.

Grains and beans (such as wheat, rice, or barley combined with pinto beans, soybeans, or lentils, etc.) form good quality proteins. Soybeans are classified as both a "complete" and a "good quality" protein food.

Research conducted by Ann Wigmore of the Hippocrates Health Institute states that sprouted grains and legumes, especially those allowed to turn green, add the additional amino acids necessary to make complete proteins of many grains and legumes.

ALL SEEDS CONTAIN ANTI-TRYPSIN INHIBITORS

All seeds contain an anti-digestant enzyme, which impairs the body's ability to digest proteins. The enzyme is a natural preservative that lasts until the proper environmental conditions bring them to life. According to Ann Wigmore, Hippocrates Diet and Health Program, soaking and sprouting leaches out this enzyme. Dr. Hal Johnson of the Food Science and Nutrition Department at Brigham Young University, Provo, Utah, 84602, maintains that only cooking destroys the enzyme and the body's ability to digest protein could be impaired if *only* uncooked sprouts were eaten for more than 1 year.

While it is unlikely any of us would have to live exclusively on sprouts for a whole year, it is a possibility that we may have to depend on them heavily until the next outdoor growing season. One family has lived exclusively on sprouts for three years and experienced improved health, with no sickness whatever during that time period. (Sprout Handbook, by Stuart Wheelwright)

SPROUTS AS A LOW-CALORIE SOURCE OF FIBER

Fiber is a popular subject these days. Because most people eat *only* refined grains, (white bread, etc.) we are constantly being encouraged to eat MORE fiber. Our bodies utilize whole foods best, so no amount of added bran or other commercially manufactured fiber food can be used by the body as efficiently as whole foods. Sprouts are whole foods, and are the most delicious, nutritious, efficient and inexpensive source of dietary fiber available.

According to the U. S. Department of Agriculture and Health and Human Services' "Nutrition and Your Health: Dietary Guidelines for Americans," "Ounce for ounce, starches (complex carbohydrates) have about half the calories of fats. Foods containing complex carbohydrates provide nutrients and dietary fiber, which is the indigestible part of plant foods. Fiber helps move foods quickly through the body."

YIELD INCREASES WHEN
GRAINS AND BEANS ARE SPROUTED

In addition to adding important enzymes, increasing nutrition, and saving time and effort in preparing whole foods, sprouting increases the yield for even greater savings on your food budget. A 15-ounce can of cooked kidney beans contains only about 4 ounces of dry beans which can be purchased for only about 15 cents. Sprouting 4 ounces of kidney beans yields over 1 1/2 pounds of beans!

Page 76

MOST POPULAR TYPES OF SEEDS

ADZUKI BEANS - Similar to the mung bean in flavor and nutrition, this small, red bean is a favorite in sprout mixes, omelets, sandwiches, or just eaten plain.

ALFALFA - In Arabic, alfalfa means "father of all food." This tender sprout is rich in vitamins A, B, C, D, E, F, and K, and in minerals such as phosphorus, iron, calcium, potassium, magnesium, sodium, silicon, and many more. According to Dr. Garnett of Stanford University, alfalfa also contains at least 8 of the essential enzymes which aid in digestion.

BARLEY - Sprouting barley adds a chewy texture to a green salad or a sprout mixture to be served as a salad. Source of iron, phosphorus, and potassium.

BUCKWHEAT - Popular as a pancake flour, whole buckwheat seed is easy to sprout and can be grown until the first leaves appear, then used as a delicious, mild salad green. Combined with alfalfa, it makes a pleasing salad base. High in vitamins A, B, C, and D.

CLOVER - A tastier cousin to alfalfa, with larger leaves. A source of calcium chromium, magnesium, phosphorous, and potassium.

GARBANZO BEANS - Naturally high in protein, this bean is my all-time favorite—either raw or cooked. It is hard to find garbanzos that will sprout, so if you find a sproutable source, buy a bunch!

MUNG BEANS - The crunchy, tasty mung bean is probably the most versatile of sprouts, and a favorite at salad bars and in many oriental recipes. Mung sprouts can be eaten after 2-3 days of sprouting, or can be sprouted under pressure for 5-7 days to produce long, juicy sprouts. Mung beans are high in calcium, magnesium, phosphorus, and vitamins A, C, and E.

KIDNEY AND PINTO BEANS - Sprouting increases the already impressive amounts of vitamins, minerals, and protein. Sprouted kidney and pinto beans make wonderful "gas-free" chili, burritos and bean dips.

LENTILS - With the flavor of freshly-ground mild black pepper, lentil sprouts are rich in iron and the B vitamins. They are delicious raw or cooked and because of their fresh, mild flavor, can be added to almost any recipe.

OATS - Sprouted oats are mild tasting and an excellent addition to soups or salads. They can be used to make an excellent sprouted grain cereal or bread.

Page 77

PEAS - Taste like fresh peas from the garden! Add to soups and stews and cook only about 2 minutes for freshest flavor. Contains vitamin C, calcium and potassium.

QUINOA - This ancient grain is noted for its high protein. It sprouts 1/4" during the 4-hour soaking process and to 1" in only one day! It's literally "bursting" with goodness! This mild sprout is excellent in salads, sandwich fillings, or just plain!

RADISH - High in potassium and vitamin C, just one single sprout has the zesty flavor of an entire garden radish.

SOYBEANS - Ounce for ounce, the soybean contains twice as much protein as meat, four times that of eggs, twelve times that of milk. A complete protein even before sprouting, it is loaded with vitamins A, B, C, E, minerals and lecithin. One-half cup of the sprouts contains as much vitamin C as 6 glasses of orange juice! Soybeans can be sprouted under pressure, like mung beans, to produce long, succulent sprouts.

SUNFLOWER - Containing up to 50% protein, sunflower sprouts are also rich in vitamins B, D, and E as well as many minerals and "good" fats. A great source of instant energy. Sprouted sunflower seeds make an excellent breakfast drink when blended with fruit or fruit juices.

WHEAT - High in vitamins B, C, E, and minerals, the vitamin E content of wheat triples during the sprouting process, making it one of man's best sources for this important vitamin. When you sprout wheat for 3 days (including soaking time) you add to the wheat: enzymes, amino acids and additional vitamins and minerals.

COMBINATIONS OF DRY SEEDS TO SPROUT TOGETHER

1) 2 T. alfalfa or clover, 4 T. mung and 1 t. radish - good in salads, sandwiches, soups and omelets

2) 2 T. mung bean, 1 T. sunflower, 2 T. lentil, 2 T. garbanzo bean - cook and mash sprouts and use as sandwich spread, in casseroles, and as the base for patties

3) 2 T. alfalfa or clover, 1/2 t. radish, 1 T. sunflower - for a lettuce replacement on sandwiches, tacos, as a border around cracked wheat or pasta salads

4) 2 T. sunflower, 2 T. lentil, 4 T. mung, 2 T. rye - good by the handful or in salads and pita pockets

HOW MUCH TO STORE?

The Benson Institute, in their booklet *Having Your Food Storage and Eating It, Too,* suggests that 370 quarts of pickled, canned, or bottled fruits and vegetables should be stored for one person for one year. (BYU Press, Provo, Utah, 84602) This is roughly 1 lb. per day per person. Does this sound like a lot? It IS! For a family of 5, this would amount to 1,850 quart jars of produce each year! Few people have access to that much produce, let alone that much storage space.

Because the volume of dry beans, peas, lentils and other seeds increases at least three to four times during the soaking and sprouting process, you would only need to store 125 pounds per person of a variety of seeds that can be sprouted and eaten raw, for fresh salads and greens, or cooked.

If you're one of the lucky few who has a fairly good supply of canned, bottled or dehydrated fruits and vegetables stored, then consider storing the following amounts for variety and better nutrition and essential enzymes:

40 pounds per person of seeds to be used in salads or as salad greens (sunflower, pumpkin, pea, alfalfa, barley, clover, buckwheat, lentil, radish, adzuki, garbanzo, quinoa, wheat, oat, and mung bean)

40 lbs. per person of seeds to sprout and use in cooking (mung, lentil, garbanzo, pinto, pink, black, kidney, small white, navy, lima, soy, etc.)

It is important to try a wide variety of sprouts and the experiment with different methods of preparing them so you will know what types your family enjoys and which ones to store. Because sprouts are such a good source of nutrition, I use them to supply necessary nutrients and consider most of the rest of our foods merely enjoyable "bulk."

In addition to bottled and dehydrated fruits and vegetables, I store the following quantities of seeds (in pounds) for sprouts to be eaten raw: sprouting barley-25, rye-15, mung beans-30, quinoa- 20, whole oats-10, alfalfa-15, peas-10, lentils-30, clover-20, sunflower-60, whole buckwheat-35.

For sprouts to be cooked, I store: Lentils-30, Garbanzo Beans-50, Pinto Beans-50, Navy or Small White Beans-50, Soy Beans-25, Mung Beans-40, Kidney Beans-20.

STORING SEEDS

Seeds should be frozen or stored in a cool, dry place in air-tight containers. Vacuum sealed or nitrogen treated seeds store the longest, with a shelf life of up to 15 years. DO NOT USE tomato or potato sprouts, or any treated seeds (usually found in the gardening section), as they are extremely poisonous. Use only untreated seeds intended for human consumption.

HOW LONG TO STORE SEEDS

There is a controversy raging about how to best store sprouting seeds. Some say "sprouting seeds need to 'breathe.' If they are stored too long in an oxygen-free environment they smother because they create their own carbon dioxide." How long is too long to store seeds without oxygen? Some people say 2 years is too long.

Recently, I tested 30-year old wheat that was stored using the dry ice method of eliminating oxygen. At the same time, I also tested 15-year old lentils packed with nitrogen. That's a long time without oxygen!! The wheat and lentils both sprouted in only 2 days, with almost 100% germination!

However, I was **unsuccessful** in sprouting seeds stored in a glass jar for only 3 years. **The key seems to be whether or not the seed will sprout when it is** *first* **purchased.** To be safe, buy a small amount and TEST the seed before purchasing and storing large quantities.

WHAT ABOUT BUGS?

One reason for taking OUT the air in stored foods is to prevent weevil and other crawley things from living in them and eating more than their share so that you end up with only hulls and carcasses.

The safest, most effective pest control for grains and small seeds that will be used for sprouting is to add diatomaceous earth (2 1/2 T. per gallon) while filling containers to distribute evenly and coat ALL the seeds. Merely pouring the powder on top and trying to stir it in does not work.

Diatomaceous earth is a white, powdery substance made up of the interior spiny skeleton of small marine creatures whose soft body parts have decomposed, leaving the remaining skeletons that accumulate on the ocean floor over thousands of years. Geological processes bring these layers to the surface where they can be mined and used for filtering systems and pest control.

It does not produce a change in taste and it is not nutritionally harmful. Besides, all traces of this fine powder are eliminated in the soaking and rinsing process of sprouting. (In fact, it is an ingredient in many toothpastes.) (*The Sense of Survival,* by J. Allan South)

A 5 lb. bag containing about 40 cups of diatomaceous earth costs only about $15. The cost of this valuable protection is only about 20¢ per 6-gallon bucket and about 4¢ per gallon!

DIRECTIONS FOR SPROUTING

Supplies needed:

🌱 **Sprouting containers.** Use *wide mouth quart jars* for alfalfa and other small leafy greens; *trays* for beans and wheatgrass, as well as buckwheat or sunflower "lettuce."

🌱 **Sprouting lids** (available at health food or preparedness stores), **fabric netting** or a piece of **fiberglass screen** to cover jar opening. (In dry climates, a piece of nylon stocking works well.)

🌱 **Sprouting seeds.** Organically grown seeds sprout the best for me. Any seed capable of growing into a plant will sprout.

The chart below will give you approximate amounts to use and how long the sprouting process should take. Times vary depending on age of seed and room temperature.

Type	Amount	Soaking Time	Sprouting Time	Yield
Alfalfa, quinoa, clover, radish, cress, or cabbage	2 T.	4 hrs.	5-7 days	2 c.
Grains, beans, peas, lentils, pumpkin, or sunflower	1/2 c.	10-12 hrs.	2-3 days	1 1/2 c.
Mung or soy (long)	1 c.	10-12 hrs.	5-6 days	4 c.
Wheat (for grass)	1 c.	10-12 hrs.	5-6 days	3 c.
Sunflower, or buck-wheat (for lettuce)	1 c.	10-12 hrs.	5-6 days	2 c.

Advance Preparation:

🌱 **BUY FRESH SEEDS AND ROTATE YOUR SEED STORAGE.** Fresh seeds tend to sprout faster and germinate better than those stored for long periods of time. Fresh seeds of all types are usually always easy to sprout, especially if they are from the current year's crop. Older seeds, especially beans, are usually slow to sprout and many in a batch will turn slimy and refuse to sprout. If you plan to buy large quantities of seeds for sprouting, ask for a sample and sprout a small amount first to test freshness. (If your stored beans or grains don't sprout, grind them to a flour and use them for thickening or baking, or cook them whole.)

🌱 **START FRESH SPROUTS OFTEN.** One of the best reasons to sprout is be able to enjoy foods that are fresh and **full** of essential nutrients. Most seeds reach maturity after 2-5 days of sprouting. The vitamin C and enzyme levels begin to decrease after that time, so start small batches of sprouts often, rather than growing a huge batch and storing it in the refrigerator. I like to start a small amount of a different seed each day, in addition to my favorites that I sprout once or twice each week. If I end up with too many sprouts to use raw, I freeze all but the green, leafy ones to use later in cooking.

Ready, Set, GO!

1. Sort and soak dry seeds. All seeds should be sorted, removing broken seeds and small pieces of debris. Place in a quart jar. Place sprouting lid or fabric (see suggestions above) over the top of the jar. If using fabric, secure with a jar ring or wide elastic band. Rinse seeds well, then pour off water and add soaking water—twice as much water as you have seeds. (Because of the excess salt in softened water, and the chlorine in city water, it is best to use purified water for soaking and rinsing.)

2. Drain well and keep moist. Whether you leave seeds in the jar or transfer to a tray, tipping the container slightly while draining will help get rid of excess water. Most failures at sprouting occur because seeds are not drained well enough. When no water drips from sprouts, roll jar so that most seeds coat sides of jar, or transfer to a sprouting tray. Remove any seeds (usually beans or peas) that have not expanded and are still hard; they will **not** sprout.

To sprout in trays, spread seeds evenly, drain well, and cover with a lid or cloth to retain moisture and keep out light.

Move jars or trays to a warm (about 70°F) place, "misting" seeds with a spray bottle one or two times a day, or enough to keep moist while sprouts reach the desired length.

Large seeds will usually need a "full bath," in running water, once each day. Small seeds, like alfalfa, usually only need a daily "misting," with a "bath" only at the end of sprouting time to wash away unsprouted seeds and hulls. The humidity and room temperature will determine "bath" frequency.

3. Harvesting. Any seed CAN be eaten when the sprout has pushed through the outer shell of the seed. Most grains and beans and larger seeds are best eaten when the sprout is as long as the seed, usually within 2-3 days.

4. "Greening." When leaves have appeared on alfalfa, and sprouts are about 1" long, place jar in a light place (not in direct sunlight) to "green" for 3-4 hours, allowing the chlorophyll to develop. Some sprouts turn bitter when they turn green, so use this method only for alfalfa, clover, radish, etc. If you like to experiment, "green" a few different kinds of sprouts and taste them to see if you like them this way.

5. "De-hulling." After "greening," put sprouts into a gallon jar or large pitcher and fill with water. The hulls will sink to the bottom or float to the top. Skim off floating hulls, then pour off water while lifting sprouts to top of the jar to allow water and hulls at the bottom of the container to pour off freely.

6. Storing Sprouts. Like any fresh vegetable, nutrients in sprouts deteriorate as soon as the sprout has reached maturity, usually within 2-3 days. Rather than grow large quantities of sprouts to store in the refrigerator for a week or more, start small quantities of fresh sprouts every few days. Check sprouts carefully, and if any mold appears on any type of sprouts, do not eat.

Store sprouted seeds in a covered container with paper toweling on the bottom and between layers. Use within 4-5 days. Sprouted beans and grains can be frozen for later use. Mung and soy beans that are sprouted to about 2" long turn limp when thawed, but can still be used in cooking.

I put 2-cup portions of sprouted grains or legumes in quart zip-loc bags, force out excess air, then stack flattened bags in the freezer where they store well for 1-2 months.

HOW TO GROW SPROUTS IN COLD WEATHER

How would you grow sprouts if you didn't have any electricity in the wintertime? What if you keep your house cooler than the recommended sprouting temperature of 70°F?

Sprouts will still grow in cold weather, but germination will be slower. In case of a power outage, you can "incubate" them by setting them in their jars or trays inside a "cooler," with 1-2 covered jars of boiling water set in the center. Place lid on top. The water may need to be reheated one or more times each day.

I usually sprout in a Rubbermaid 12-gallon tub with a lid. It's just the right size for all my jars and trays and it keeps my counters uncluttered when I'm sprouting lots of different kinds of seeds. If you have an exceptionally cold house, a heavy cardboard box wrapped in a mylar blanket or covered with heavy foil will also work well to provide a warmer sprouting environment.

SPROUTING MUNG AND SOYBEANS UNDER PRESSURE

Supplies:

- ❧ Gallon metal or plastic container (large enough to hold sprout container)

- ❧ Plastic 2-quart container with drainage holes in sides and bottom

- ❧ Burlap fabric to fold and place on top of soaked seeds

- ❧ 3-5 pounds small washed rocks or marbles

- ❧ Burlap or Muslin bag to hold rocks or marbles

- ❧ Lid to cover containers

Mung and soybeans can be sprouted under pressure to produce long, fat, succulent sprouts 2-3" long—just like the ones in the grocery store.

Soak 1 c. seeds for 12 to 18 hours. Pour soaked seeds into the plastic container. Cover with several layers of burlap (to help keep sprouts moist and dark). Place rocks or marbles in cloth bag on top of soaked seeds.

Put this container inside the gallon metal or plastic container (to maintain constant temperature and moisture, and to keep out all light). Cover both containers with a thick cloth. These sprouts must be kept in the dark at all times or they turn green and taste bitter.

Water 3-4 times a day so roots do not grow long and skinny looking for water. Or, if drainage is good and sprouts can be kept dark, cover with a towel and leave under a dripping faucet (lukewarm water) for most of the day.

GROWING WHEAT GRASS, BUCKWHEAT AND SUNFLOWER SEEDS

The easiest way to grow wheat grass, sunflower seeds, or buckwheat lettuce (to harvest as salad greens) is to spread a thick layer (seeds touching) of barely sprouted grain or seeds on top of several layers of damp paper toweling on a tray or screen. Cover with eight layers of wet newspaper, then cover with a layer of plastic (a garbage bag works well). Put in a warm, dark place for 2 days.

Remove paper and plastic and water lightly if dry. Rinse or sprinkle with lukewarm water 2 times a day for 3 more days. Cover loosely.

Shoots will start to turn green in normal household light. Expose shoots to indirect sunlight after 5 days so they will turn dark green.

Wheat grass grows straight and tall, like regular grass. Sunflower and buckwheat seeds will sprout two green leaves. Grass, stems and leaves can be used (everything down to the roots) to make nutritious drinks, salads, sandwiches, or for eating plain.

SPROUTING LARGE QUANTITIES OF VARIOUS BEANS AND SEEDS

Supplies needed:

Large colander
Bowl large enough to hold colander
15″ square of cheesecloth or cotton
  muslin for each type of sprout
Dishtowel to cover bowl and to
  keep sprouts warm and dark

If you want to sprout wheat, lentils, or beans for quantity cooking, freezing, or demonstrations, the easiest way is to put 1 cup of each different type of soaked seeds into a 15″ square of fabric. Twist ends together loosely and place all into a colander and then inside a large bowl. Cover with a towel.

Four or five bags in a colander is ideal, as they keep each other warm. These need to be kept in a warm, dark place and rinsed 2-3 times a day with lukewarm water.

To rinse, open bags of sprouts and rinse under lukewarm running water. Put bags back into colander, then into the bowl and cover again. No draining time is necessary because seeds continue to drain after the colander has been put inside the larger bowl.

Seeds will sprout enough in 2-3 days to be used in cooking.

POPULAR USES FOR SPROUTS

Since many vitamins, minerals, and enzymes are destroyed in cooking, try to use the tender raw sprouts in uncooked recipes whenever possible, or add to cooked foods just before serving.

DRINKS: Sunflower, alfalfa, buckwheat and wheat sprouts can be blended into fruit drinks and shakes.

OMELETS: Mung, lentil, sunflower, garbanzo, or sunflower sprouts can be added to scrambled eggs or omelets.

STIR FRY: Mung and soy bean, lentil, garbanzo and sunflower sprouts can be sauteed with other vegetables or added at the last minute.

PANCAKES: Wheat, buckwheat, chopped alfalfa and sunflower seeds can be mixed with batter or added after pancake has been poured onto griddle.

BREADS: Wheat, alfalfa, sunflower, buckwheat, rye, oats can be added to batter before baking.

SALADS: Alfalfa, lentil, mung, garbanzo, wheat, radish, sunflower or mixed sprouts can be added to tossed salads, wheat or pasta salads, or three bean salads. Wheat sprouts are sweet and taste great in fruit salads.

DESSERTS: Wheat (sprouted 3 days so it turns sweet) and sunflower seeds (sprouted 1/8" or less) are good in peanut butter candies and in ground nut and raisin balls.

SPROUT BREAKFASTS

Breakfasts that are full of fiber are guaranteed to fill you full for longer! With the addition of sprouts, breakfast can be a very satisfying, nutritious meal.

In this section, you will find sprouts in good-for-you drinks, eggs, cereals and muffins.

HIGH-FIBER BREAKFAST DRINKS

SUNSHAKE

6 oz. frozen apple juice
1/2 c. dry milk powder
2 frozen bananas or other fruit
1/2 c. sprouted sunflower seeds

1 c. water
1 t. vanilla
8 ice cubes

Blend sprouts, water and apple juice concentrate until smooth. Add chunks of bananas, milk powder, vanilla and ice cubes (one at a time). Serve immediately You can add or substitute other fruits or berries if available. Serves 4.

With juice, fruit and milk used in this shake, we often eat a piece of toast (or even a healthy cookie) and call it breakfast!

Cal. 180 **Fat** 3g/13% **Carb.** 6g **Fbr.** 2g **Pro.** 6g

CHERRY PROTEIN DELIGHT

1/2 c. ground sesame seeds
1 1/2 c. water
2 c. frozen cherries
1 T. vanilla

2 T. sprouted sunflower seeds
4 bananas, fresh or frozen
6 ice cubes
1/2 c. frozen apple juice concentrate

Blend well and serve. Serves 6.

Cal. 180 **Fat** 4g/19% **Carb.** 34g **Fbr.** 3g **Pro.** 3g

PINEAPPLE FREEZE

2 c. pineapple juice
2 t. vanilla
1/4 c. sprouted sunflower seeds
2 ripe bananas

2 c. yogurt
1/2 c. dry milk powder
16 oz. frozen apple juice concentrate
1 c. frozen orange juice concentrate

Blend all ingredients about 2 minutes in blender. Serve immediately or pour into an 8" baking dish a freeze until firm. When ready to serve, cut into chunks and blend, adding water or fruit juice to make a thick, creamy shake. Serves 6.

Cal. 226 **Fat** 1.2g/5% **Carb.** 45g **Fbr.** 1g **Pro.** 5g

EGGS AND SPROUTS

SCRAMBLED EGGS WITH SPROUTS

4 eggs
1/2 c. chopped lentil sprouts
1/2 c. cooked cracked wheat
  or brown rice

1/2 c. chopped onions
1/2 t. chicken-flavored bouillon
1/4 c. grated low-fat cheese (opt.)

Mix all but cheese and pour into hot skillet coated with cooking spray. Stir and cook until almost set. Top with cheese and serve immediately. Serves 4. Note: Substitute mung or soy bean sprouts for lentils.

Cal. 114 **Fat** .8g/6% **Carb.** 17g **Fbr.** 4g **Pro.** 10g

EGGS OLÉ

1 green chile, diced
1 tomato, diced
2 T. water
1/2 c. cooked brown rice
1/8 t. garlic powder
1 c. chopped mung bean sprouts

4 eggs
1/4 c. water
1 T. dry milk powder
1 t. dry minced onion
salt and pepper to taste

In a medium skillet, steam chilies, sprouts and tomato in 2 T. water for 1 minute. In a medium bowl, beat together remaining ingredients. Add steamed vegetables. Coat pan with cooking spray and pour in egg mixture. Cook over medium heat for 2 minutes until partially set. With a fork, gently stir and turn until firm. If desired, sprinkle with 1/2 c. cheddar cheese and minced fresh parsley. Serves 4.

Cal. 116 **Fat** .5g/3% **Carb.** 21g **Fbr.** 2g **Pro.** 6g

FLUFFY SPROUT OMELET

4 egg yolks, lightly beaten
2 T. dry milk powder
1/4 t. salt

1/4 c. water
1/2 c. grated fat-free cheese
1 c. chopped mung bean sprouts
4 egg whites, beaten stiff

Mix egg yolks, milk, salt and cheese. Fold in egg whites and sprouts. Coat a large frying pan with cooking spray. Pour all of omelet mixture into the pan, cover and cook over low heat until firm. Fold omelet over and lift out whole, or cut into sections. If desired, top with more sprouts, grated cheese, or Picante sauce. Serves 4.

Cal. 50 **Fat** .1g/1% **Carb.** 2g **Fbr.** 1g **Pro.** 9g

CEREALS

HOT CRACKED OATS

1 c. cracked oats
1 3/4 c. water

1/2 c. sprouted wheat

In a small saucepan over medium heat, bring water and oats to a boil, stirring occasionally. Turn off heat, cover pan and let sit 15 minutes. Top with 3-day sprouted wheat. If desired, add raisins and/or ground nuts. Serves 4.

Cal. 101 **Fat** 1.4g/12% **Carb.** 19g **Fbr.** 2g **Pro.** 4g

FRESH FRUIT 'N OATMEAL

2 c. rolled oats, soaked overnight in 2 c. water
1/2 c. ground almonds (opt.)
1/4 c. honey
1 c. sprouted sunflower seeds

1/4 c. fresh lemon juice
8 c. grated apples

Mix all together and top with additional chopped almonds, if desired. Sprinkle with cinnamon and/or nutmeg. Serves 8.

Cal. 100 **Fat** 1.9g/16% **Carb.** 20g **Fbr.** 3g **Pro.** 2g

HEARTY OATMEAL

2 c. rolled oats　　　　　　　*4 c. water*
1/2 c. dates/raisins　　　　　*1/4 t. salt (opt)*
1/2 c. sprouted wheat

Combine sprouts and raisins or dates with water and heat to boiling. Add oats and salt. Take off heat and cover. Let sit 10 minutes. Stir and serve with honey, butter and a dash of cinnamon. If you like milk on your cereal, mix 3/4 c. dry non-instant milk with the oats before adding to the boiling water. This will prevent lumping. Rolled wheat can be substituted for rolled oats. Serves 4. Note: Oatmeal cooks faster than rolled oats (which are simply oats that are rolled), so if you only have oatmeal, let sit only 5 minutes.

Cal. 162 **Fat** 1.9g/10% **Carb.** 33g **Fbr.** 4g **Pro.** 5g

THERMOS WHEAT SPROUTS

2 c. 2-day wheat sprouts　　　　*4 c. boiling water*

Put 2 c. boiling water into a 1 quart glass or metal lined thermos to preheat for 5 minutes. Put wheat sprouts and remaining water into thermos, cap tightly and let sit for at least 1 hour. This is best when made at night for a quick, easy breakfast. When left overnight, the kernels pop open and are very easy to chew.

Cal. 105 **Fat** .6g/5% **Carb.** 22g **Fbr.** 4g **Pro.** 5g

Nest Cooking - If you do not have access to a thermos, use a gallon can or bottle. Use 4 c. sprouts and 4 c. boiling water, or 4 c. dry wheat (rinsed) and 8 c. boiling water. Pour wheat and water into can or bottle and put a tight-fitting lid. Put the can into a two-piece apple box tightly stuffed with crumbled newspapers, blankets, or rags. Put lid on box and let sit 10-12 hours. Wheat kernels will pop open and be steaming hot.

Cal. 105 **Fat** .6g/5% **Carb.** 22g **Fbr.** 4g **Pro.** 5g

MUFFINS

SPROUT MUFFINS

2 c. whole wheat flour
1/3 c. honey or brown sugar
1/4 c. applesauce
1 c. chopped alfalfa sprouts
1 c. water

1 egg, well beaten
2 t. baking powder
1/2 t. salt
2 T. dry milk powder

Put dry ingredients and sprouts into a mixing bowl and stir well. Make a nest in the center of flour mixture and add egg, honey, applesauce and water. Mix only until flour is moistened. Spoon into muffin tins coated with cooking spray or use paper muffin cups. Fill 2/3 full. Bake at 400°F for 25 minutes. Makes 1 dozen muffins.

Cal 108 Fat .4g/3% Carb 27g Fbr 3g Pro 4g

OAT BRAN ORANGE MUFFINS

2 c. oat bran cereal, uncooked
1/2 c. pinto bean flour
2 t. baking powder
2 T. buttermilk powder
2 T. grated orange rind
1/2 t. salt (opt.)

1/2 c. raisins
1/4 c. honey
1/2 c. apple juice concentrate
1 c. orange juice
1/4 c. 3-day sprouted wheat
2 egg whites, beaten stiff

Combine all dry ingredients. Make a nest and stir in remaining ingredients, folding in egg whites last. Fill muffin tins coated with baking spray 2/3 full and bake at 400° 15-20 minutes. Makes 6 lg. muffins.

Cal. 80 **Fat** .5g/5% **Carb.** 20g **Fbr.** 5g **Pro.** 4g

SPROUT SALADS

Since green vegetables contain amino acids, they form a perfect protein when combined with wheat. Fresh vegetables are often expensive and sometimes unavailable, so sprouting seeds and equipment should be an important part of any well-stocked pantry.

One half cup mung bean sprouts supplies the recommended daily allowance of vitamin C, so add your favorite sprouts to every salad.

COLD NOODLE SALAD

2 cups cooked linguini noodles,   *1/4 c. shredded carrot*
2 cups 3" long mung bean sprouts   *1 green onion, chopped*
1/2 c. cooked brown rice, cooled   *1/2 c. finely diced celery*

Layer cooled noodles and other ingredients in order given and add soy sauce or Peanut Sauce (see below) to taste.

Cal. 162 **Fat** .9g/5% **Carb.** 34g **Fbr.** 3g **Pro.** 6g

AVEY'S PEANUT SAUCE

1/4 c. soy sauce   *1/2 t. salt*
2 T. seasoned rice vinegar   *3/4 t. powdered ginger***
1/2 c. water   *1 t. minced garlic*
2 T. honey   *1/3 c. crunchy peanut butter*
2 T. sesame oil*

Place all ingredients in a small saucepan. Stir with a wire whip and cook over medium heat for 1 minute, or until thick. Cool to serve. Stores well in refrigerator. *Note: HOT sesame oil (seasoned with hot peppers) is excellent in this dish.

**If available, use 1-2 T. peeled, grated fresh ginger or more ZING.

Cal. 52 **Fat** 4.2g/69% **Carb.** 3g **Fbr.** 1g **Pro.** 1g per T.

ZUCCHINI SALAD

1 c. 2-day sunflower sprouts   *1 T. sesame seeds*
2 c. shredded zucchini   *1 c. sliced mushrooms*
1 c. finely sliced celery   *1/2 c. fat-free mayonnaise*
1 t. chicken-flavored bouillon   *1/4 c. mild Picante sauce*

Mix bouillon, mayonnaise and picante sauce. Combine remaining ingredients and serve on lettuce and/or sprout-lined plates. Top with dressing and serve immediately. (The salt content in the bouillon makes the zucchini "weep" if it stands for more than 1/2 hour. If salad is to be mixed ahead of time, add 1/8 t. salt to zucchini and let drain for 15 minutes, then squeeze out liquid, before adding remaining ingredients.) Serves 4. Excellent over cold rice!

Cal. 114 **Fat** 6.6g/50% **Carb.** 10.6g **Fbr.** 3g **Pro.** 5g

GREEN EGGS 'N GRAINS

1 c. cooked cracked wheat
1/2 c. cooked brown rice
3 hard boiled eggs, chopped
2 T. chopped green onions
1/8 t. prepared mustard

2 T. chopped olives
1 t. chopped parsley
1 T. chicken-flavored bouillon
4 T. fat-free mayonnaise
16 oz. pkg. frozen peas

Slightly thaw and drain peas, then add remaining ingredients. Serve cold as a sandwich filling or salad. Serves 6.

Cal. 149 **Fat** 3.3g/20% **Carb.** 22g **Fbr.** 5g **Pro.** 9g

CURRIED RICE SALAD

2 c. cooked brown rice
1 c. diced celery
1/2 t. curry powder
2 T. chopped onions

2 t. beef-flavored bouillon
1/2 c. fat-free cottage cheese
1/3 c. fat-free mayonnaise
1 c. alfalfa sprouts for garnish

Mix all ingredients except sprouts together and serve. Top with sprouts and freshly diced tomatoes or shredded cheese, if desired. This is also an excellent pita bread filling. Serves 4.

Cal. 131 **Fat** 2.7g/7% **Carb.** 27g **Fbr.** 2g **Pro.** 3g

SPROUT SALAD

1 large bunch chopped lettuce
1 diced cucumber
1 c. mung bean sprouts
2 T. lentil sprouts

1 c. alfalfa sprouts
1 grated carrot
1 lg. diced tomato

Lightly toss all but alfalfa sprouts. Garnish with sprouts or freshly chopped chives. Top with your favorite dressing. Serves 6.

Cal. 118 **Fat** .6g/4% **Carb.** 25g **Fbr.** 6g **Pro.** 5g

BASIC GREEN SALAD
OR SANDWICH FILLING

2 cups of one or more of the following greens:

romaine lettuce   *spinach*
bib lettuce   *swiss chard*
boston lettuce   *beet greens (young)*
red leaf lettuce

Add color and nutrition with 2 cups of:

sprouts - try alfalfa, radish, mung, sunflower, or wheat
raw broccoli pieces   *radishes*
raw cauliflower pieces   *red or green cabbage*
bell pepper   *celery*
avocado   *carrots*
beets   *peas*
tomato   *grated fat-free cheese*

Tear 2 c. greens and slice, chop or grate 2 c. of a variety of the other sprouts and vegetables. Top with sprouted or toasted sunflower seeds.

Serve with Ranch or Thousand Island Dressing. Serves 4.

HEARTY SPROUT STIR-FRY SALAD

3 T. vegetable broth   *1 t. chicken-flavored bouillon*
1/2 c. shredded carrots   *1/2 t. ginger powder*
1/2 onion, shredded   *1-2 T. soy sauce*
1 c. mung bean sprouts   *1 c. cooked wheat*
1 c. celery, diced   *1 c. frozen peas*

Heat broth in skillet. Add carrots, onion, sprouts and celery and cook 2-3 minutes, adding more water, as needed, to cook to the tender/crunchy stage. Chill 15 minutes. Add remaining ingredients and mix well. Can be served over chilled rice or salad greens. Serves 6.

Cal. 118 **Fat** .6g/7% **Carb.** 25g **Fbr.** 7g **Pro.** 5g

HAWAIIAN COLE SLAW

4 c. shredded cabbage
1 c. crushed pineapple
1 T. honey

3/4 c. fat-free mayonnaise
1 c. 2-day wheat sprouts

Add drained pineapple to other ingredients. If you like a sweet salad, you can add 1/4 c. raisins and a little shredded coconut. Serve cold. Serves 6.

Cal. 156 **Fat** .6g/3% **Carb.** 39g **Fbr.** 3g **Pro.** 3g

CUCUMBER AND SPROUT SALAD

1 cucumber, diced
4 tomatoes, diced
1 c. alfalfa or clover sprouts

Salad greens
French or Ranch dressing

Mix cucumber and tomatoes and place on a bed of fresh salad greens, surrounded by alfalfa sprouts, and topped with French or Ranch dressing. This is also good with sprouted or toasted sesame seeds. Serves 6.

Cal. 30 **Fat** .4g/11% **Carb.** 6g **Fbr.** 2g **Pro.** 2g

GARBANZO BEAN SALAD

2 c. sprouted garbanzo beans
1 c. chopped mung bean sprouts
2 t. fresh parsley, chopped
1/4 c. chopped green onion

1 diced cucumber
1 chopped tomato
1 c. chopped celery
French dressing

Steam garbanzo bean sprouts until tender/crunchy. Cool and mix with other ingredients. Chill and serve with Sweet and Sour Sauce or Ranch dressing. Serves 4. Sprinkle with sesame seeds, if desired.

Cal. 214 **Fat** 3.2g/13% **Carb.** 37g **Fbr.** 2g **Pro.** 12g

ORIENTAL PASTA SALAD

1/2 lb. spiral noodles
1 rib celery, sliced
2 c. mung bean sprouts

1/2 c. cooked cracked wheat
1/2 c. each - green onions,
  tomatoes, green peppers, broccoli
parsley for garnish

Cook pasta according to package directions. Rinse in cold water, drain. Combine pasta with wheat, celery and sprouts. Place on serving tray. Arrange remaining vegetables in layers or rings on top of pasta mixture. Top with dressing (or sprinkle with rice vinegar and sesame oil. Serves 6.

Cal. 157 **Fat** .7g/4% **Carb.** 34g **Fbr.** 2g **Pro.** 7g

ORIENTAL PASTA SALAD DRESSING

1/2 c. chicken broth
2 T. soy sauce
1 1/2 t. ginger
1 1/2 t. mustard

1/4 c. Sweet and Sour Sauce
  (see page 21)
1 T. sesame seeds

MUNG BEAN SPROUT SALAD

1 c. mung bean sprouts
1 c. fresh or frozen peas
1 c. coarsely grated carrots
2 c. buckwheat sprout "lettuce" or shredded head lettuce

1 c. chopped celery
1 lg. diced cucumber
1 T. sesame seeds

Toss lightly and top with dressing of your choice. Serves 4.

Cal. 73 **Fat** .9g/10% **Carb.** 14g **Fbr.** 5g **Pro.** 4g

SUPER EASY SUN SALAD

2 c. 2-3 day sprouted sunflower seeds
1 T. lemon juice
1 t. olive oil

Mix all ingredients (add salt to taste) and serve plain or on a bed of lettuce or sprouts. Serves 4.

Cal. 113 **Fat** 10g/74% **Carb.** 4g **Fbr.** 2g **Pro.** 4g

SIDE DISHES

These recipes make a perfect complement to a filling main dish. OR, serve Side Dishes with a large salad and a hot vegetable for a complete meal.

Sprouted beans, grains and seeds add variety as well as nutrition and fiber to any recipe, so try adding them to your favorite family recipes.

BEAN SPROUT OMELET IN A WRAPPER

4 flour tortillas or crepes
4 eggs or 8 egg whites
1 T. Picante sauce
2 T. dry milk powder

1 c. mung bean sprouts, chopped
1 c. grated fat-free cheese
1 t. parsley

Brown tortillas or crepes in a dry, heavy skillet. Blend eggs, Picante sauce and dry milk. Pour into a skillet coated with cooking spray and cook like a regular omelet. Cut into 4 strips and fill each flour tortilla or crepe. Top with cheese and sprouts, roll up and put back in pan. Cover and simmer over very low heat (or use microwave) to melt cheese. Serve hot, sprinkled with a little fresh or dried parsley. Serves 4.

Cal. 194 **Fat** 2.6g/12% **Carb.** 24g **Fbr.** 2g **Pro.** 19g

TORTILLA MUNCHIES

6 whole wheat tortillas
1/2 c. sprouted sunflower seeds
1/2 c. cooked cracked wheat
1/4 c. chopped green onions

1/2 c. Picante sauce
1 c. grated fat-free cheese
1/3 c. fat-free mayonnaise
1 t. beef-flavored bouillon

Mix all ingredients except tortillas. Heat tortillas in a skillet coated with cooking spray. Spread about 1/2 c. mixture on each tortilla, cover, and heat through. Roll or fold, cut into bite-sized pieces and serve. Top with additional cheese, if desired. Serves 6.

Cal. 179 **Fat** 4g/20% **Carb.** 27g **Fbr.** 2g **Pro.** 9g

POTATO PATTIES

1 c. sprouted garbanzo beans
3 lg. potatoes, cooked and mashed
1 T. poultry seasoning
1/4 t. ea. onion and garlic powder

3 eggs or 6 egg whites
2 c. chopped mushrooms
2 T. parmesan cheese
1 T. Picante sauce

Chop sprouted beans, mix with remaining ingredients and spoon into a hot skillet coated with cooking spray. Cover and cook over medium heat until browned on both sides. Serves 6.

Cal. 259 **Fat** 2.7g/9% **Carb.** 49g **Fbr.** 12g **Pro.** 12g

CARROT SQUARES

6 large carrots, grated
3 green onions, chopped
4 eggs or 8 egg whites
1 c. water
1 T. chicken-flavored bouillon
1 c. cooked cracked wheat

1/2 t. pepper
1 T. parsley
1 c. fat-free cottage cheese
3 T. dry milk powder
3 T. sunflower sprouts
3/4 c. alfalfa sprouts

Simmer grated carrots and chopped onions 3 minutes in 1/4 c. of the water. Blend eggs, remaining water, dry milk and seasonings until frothy. Add carrots and onions. Mix well and add cottage cheese, cracked wheat and alfalfa sprouts. Pour into 9 x 13" baking dish coated with cooking spray. Sprinkle with sunflower sprouts. Bake 25-30 minutes at 350°F or until set and lightly browned on edges. Cut in squares. Serve hot or cold. Serves 8.

Cal. 107 **Fat** .9g/7% **Carb.** 16g **Fbr.** 4g **Pro.** 10g

SPROUTED WHEAT BALLS

2 c. sprouted wheat
1/2 c. sprouted sunflower seeds
1 lg. onion, chopped
2 T. red or brown lentil flour
1 T. dried parsley
2 T. Picante Sauce

1 T. beef-flavored bouillon
2 c. wheat bread crumbs
1 t. cumin
3 T. dry milk powder
***
1 c. water

Put mixed sprouted wheat, sunflower seeds and onion through the fine blade of a meat grinder or food processor. Put into a bowl and add all remaining ingredients and enough water to make a mixture that holds together. Form into 1" balls or 2" patties and fry or steam in heavy skillet until golden brown on both sides. Serves 6-8. These may also be topped with cheese and broiled.

Cal. 191 **Fat** 4.4g/21% **Carb.** 32g **Fbr.** 2g **Pro.** 6g

SPROUT SOUPS

Many sprouted beans will cook in 30 minutes or less. A good way to make fast bean soups is to sprout beans for 2-3 days (with the sprout being as long as the bean), then freeze in 2 cup portions in zip-loc bags. Thaw in the boiling water called for in each soup.

CREAMY SPROUT SOUP (FOUR STARS!!****)

4 c. boiling water
4 t. chicken-flavored bouillon
1/2 c. cooked wheat
3 eggs, well beaten, or 6 egg whites

2 c. sprouted navy beans
1 t. dried parsley
1 c. shredded potatoes
1/4 c. chopped mushrooms

To boiling water, add all but eggs, wheat and mushrooms. You can use whole or cracked wheat, and a variety of sprouted beans. Cook until potatoes and bean sprouts are tender, about 15 minutes. (The beans should be more firm than mushy.) Mix eggs, mushrooms, wheat and a small amount of hot soup. Stir slowly into soup and cook an additional 4 minutes. Do not boil. Serves 6-8.

Cal. 125 **Fat** .5g/3% **Carb.** 35g **Fbr.** 10g **Pro.** 12g

SPROUTED LENTIL SOUP

4 c. boiling water
4 c. lentil sprouts
2 grated carrots
1 T. beef-flavored bouillon

1 chopped onion
2 large chopped tomatoes
2 stalks chopped celery
salt and pepper to taste

Add all ingredients to boiling water and bring back to a boil. Cover and cook over low heat 15 minutes. Serves 6.

Cal. 80 **Fat** 4.4g/5% **Carb.** 17g **Fbr.** 1g **Pro.** 6g

SPROUTED SOYBEAN SOUP

5 c. boiling water
2 c. 1" sprouted soybeans
1 T. dry parsley
1 c. grated potatoes
1 c. chopped green onion tops

1 chopped onion
1 grated carrot
2 T. chicken-flavored bouillon
salt and pepper to taste

Cook soybeans until crunchy/tender in boiling water (about 15 minutes). Add remaining ingredients and cook over low heat 20 minutes. Thicken, if desired with 4 T. cornstarch mixed in 1/2 c. warm water. Serves 6.

Cal. 88 **Fat** 1.7g/15% **Carb.** 15g **Fbr.** 2g **Pro.** 5g

CREAMY POTATO LENTIL SOUP

1 c. lentil sprouts
4 c. boiling water
2 c. grated potato

1 T. chicken or beef-flavored bouillon
3/4 c. dry milk powder
salt and pepper to taste

Cook potatoes in seasoned water until tender, about 10 minutes. Blend until smooth, using a small amount of the liquid. Add sprouts, more water and dry milk powder; blend again until smooth. Heat just to the boiling point, season to taste. Serves 4.

Cal. 195 **Fat** .2g/1% **Carb.** 41g **Fbr.** 3g **Pro.** 9g

VEGETABLE BEAN SOUP

1 lg. chopped onion
1 diced green pepper
2 c. bottled tomatoes
2 qt. boiling water

4 lg. grated carrots
1 T. chicken or vegetable bouillon
3 c. sprouted white beans
1/4 c. cornstarch

Bring all but cornstarch to a boil and simmer 20-30 minutes, stirring occasionally. Mix cornstarch with 1 c. warm water and slowly pour into cooked soup, stirring constantly. Cook about 1 minute until thickened. Serves 6.

Cal. 179 **Fat** .6g/3% **Carb.** 36g **Fbr.** 12g **Pro.** 7g

POTATO-BEAN SOUP THICKENER

1/2 c. white bean flour
1/2 c. potato flour
1/3 c. red lentil flour
1/2 t. onion powder

1/4 t. garlic powder
1/4 t. ground celery seed
1/4 t. black pepper (opt.)
1 1/2 t. salt (opt.)

Use to thicken any soup, as you would flour or cornstarch. Example: Combine 6 c. hot chicken or vegetable broth, 3 c. grated or finely chopped veggies and 1 c. uncooked pasta noodles, and cook until pasta is tender. Whisk in 1/2 cup Potato-Bean Thickener. Bring to a boil, then reduce heat and simmer 2 minutes.

Cal. 57 **Fat** .1g/2.3% **Carb.** 12g **Fbr.** 2g **Pro.** 3g

SOUPER SPROUT BEAN SOUP

6 c. boiling water
2 c. sprouted white beans
1 c. sprouted peas
1 c. sprouted lentils

1 c. sprouted wheat
1 46 oz. can tomato juice
2 qt. bottled tomatoes
3 T. beef-flavored bouillon

(Frozen sprouts are most convenient to use here. You can chop or coarsely grind sprouted peas and beans for faster cooking.) Bring all ingredients to a boil and simmer about 15 minutes. (The finer you cut vegetables, the quicker they cook.)

2 c. onions, grated
1 c. carrots, grated
2 c. celery, finely diced

1 c. cabbage, chopped fine
1/8 t. marjoram
1 t. cumin

Cook until carrots are tender - about 5 minutes. If desired, add 2 c. fresh or frozen peas about 1 minute before the end of cooking time. Serves 6.

Cal. 167 **Fat** 1.3g/7% **Carb.** 34g **Fbr.** 10g **Pro.** 8g

SUPER SPROUT CHILI

6 oz. cooked kidney bean sprouts
1 c. cooked wheat sprouts
3 8 oz. cans tomato sauce
1 6 oz. can tomato paste
2 c. chopped onions
4 oz. can chopped olives

1 lg. chopped green pepper
2 c. bottled tomatoes
2 T. chili powder
2 T. powdered cumin
3 T. beef-flavored bouillon
salt and pepper to taste

Combine all ingredients and cook over medium heat 25 minutes. If thicker chili is desired, stir 4 T. cornstarch into 1/2 c. water. Stir into cooked bean mixture. Simmer until thickened, about 3 minutes. Serves 8.

Cal. 287 **Fat** 3.6g/10% **Carb.** 53g **Fbr.** 13g **Pro.** 16g

MAIN DISH MEALS

Whether you're cooking for 2 or for a crowd, these full-of-fiber main dishes with flavors from Mexico, China and Italy are sure to please.

Grains and beans, sprouted and cooked, are combined with fresh vegetables to form high-protein meals that will fill your nutritional needs.

MEXICAN BEAN CASSEROLE

1 c. water or bean liquid	1 T. beef-flavored bouillon
1 finely chopped onion	1/2 t. garlic powder
3 c. sprouted pinto beans	1 1/2 c. taco or Picante sauce
1 1/2 t. cumin	1/2 t. salt
1 1/2 t. chili powder	1 c. cooked cracked wheat

Cook onions in 1/4 c. water or bean liquid for 2 minutes. Add to hot, cooked beans (can be sprouted, cooked, frozen, then reheated). Then mix in all remaining ingredients. Bake in a 2 quart casserole at 350°F for 20-30 minutes, until center of casserole is bubbly. Makes 5 cups. (Also good as a chip dip.)

Cal. 230 **Fat** 1g/4% **Carb.** 41g **Fbr.** 12g **Pro.** 17g

SAUTÉED BEAN SPROUTS

3 T. vegetable broth	1/2 c. cooked cracked wheat or rice
2 green onions, chopped	1/4 t. ginger
3 c. mung or soy bean sprouts	1 T. chicken-flavored bouillon
1/3 c. water chestnuts or sliced celery	1 T. soy sauce

Heat broth, add onion and cook 30 seconds. Add sprouts and cook, stirring for 1 minute. If mixture begins to stick, add a tablespoon of water at a time, only enough to continue the cooking. Add remaining ingredients. Cover and cook for 4 minutes. Serve hot as a side dish, or over a wheat and rice combination (1/2 and 1/2, cooked together) for a main dish. Serves 4.

Cal. 96 **Fat** .7g/6% **Carb.** 20g **Fbr.** 4g **Pro.** 5g

NON-CHICKEN CHOW MEIN

2 T. water or oil
1 c. sliced mushrooms
2 c. water
1 T. chicken-flavored bouillon
2 t. cornstarch
2 c. cooked cracked wheat

2 lg. onions, chopped
3 c. chopped celery or
  Chinese cabbage
2 t. soy sauce
1 c. mung bean sprouts

Cook onions and celery for 1 minute in water or oil over medium high heat. Add sprouts and mushrooms and cook 2 minutes more, adding more water if necessary. Mix cornstarch, soy sauce and bouillon in 1/4 c. water and stir into vegetable mixture. Cook only until thickened, about 30 seconds. Serve hot over cracked wheat, or a combination of wheat and rice. Serves 6.

Cal. 191 **Fat** 4.4g/21% **Carb.** 32g **Fbr.** 2g **Pro.** 6g

SPROUT FILLED WON TONS

18 small won ton wrappers
1 c. sprouted mung beans
1 c. shredded cabbage
1 c. chopped green onions
2 c. cooked cracked wheat

2 T. soy sauce
2 egg whites
1/8 t. ginger
2 t. chicken-flavored bouillon
cooking spray for cooking

Mix all ingredients and place 1 teaspoon filling in the center of each wrapper. Moisten all edges with water. Fold corner over, forming a triangle, and tuck edges under filled wrapper. Fry 2-3 minutes in hot skillet coated with cooking spray. Then add 1/2 c. water, cover and steam 15-20 minutes). Serve plain or with Sweet and Sour Sauce (see recipe on Page 22). Serves 6.

Cal. 149 **Fat** 1.3g/8% **Carb.** 28g **Fbr.** 4g **Pro.** 7g

ITALIAN WHEAT RING

1 c. spaghetti or tomato sauce
1 T. dried minced onion
1 c. cooked cracked wheat
1 c. chopped mung bean sprouts
1/2 lb. fat-free cottage cheese
1/4 t. each oregano, thyme, marjoram

3/4 c. oatmeal
4 T. chopped olives
2 egg whites
1/4 t. salt
1/4 c. Parmesan cheese

Set aside 1/2 of cheese and olives. Mix all remaining ingredients and pour into a 1 quart ring mold or 6 large muffin tins, coated with cooking spray. Bake at 375°F for 25 minutes or until set. Top with remaining cheese and olives and put back in oven to melt cheese. Serves 4.

Cal. 225 **Fat** 3.7g/14% **Carb.** 28g **Fbr.** 5g **Pro.** 23g

ENCHILADA CASSEROLE

1 T. beef-flavored bouillon
1 c. chopped onions
1/2 t. oregano
2 T. chili powder
3 1/2 c. water
3/4 c. wheat flour

1 c. tomato sauce
1 c. cooked cracked wheat
12 corn tortillas
2 c. cooked, sprouted beans
2 c. fat-free cottage cheese

Add onions and seasonings to water and simmer 3 minutes. Stir in tomato sauce, wheat and flour mixture and heat through.   In a 9"x13" pan coated with cooking spray, layer sauce, corn tortillas and cheese, ending with cheese on top. Bake at 350°F for 15 minutes, or until heated through. Serves 6-9.

Cal. 247 **Fat** 1.6g/6% **Carb.** 42g **Fbr.** 8g **Pro.** 20g

SPROUT SNACKS
AND DESSERTS

Adding sprouts to snacks and desserts ensures an extra dose of fiber and nutrition.

Cooking destroys some of the fiber and nutrients, so use uncooked sprouts as often as possible.

Sprouting nutritious nuts and seeds makes them easier to digest...especially helpful for young children.

Milks made from sprouted nuts and seeds make an excellent base for super-nutritious shakes. Add dates or honey and fresh or frozen fruits and frozen fruit juice concentrates for power-packed snacks.

HOT BEAN DIP (REFRIED BEANS)

1/2 med. onion, minced   *1/2 t. garlic powder*
1/2 t. cumin   *1/2 t. salt*
1 c. fat-free cottage cheese   *3 c. sprouted pinto beans*

Cook beans until tender. (Pressure cook 5 min. at 10 lb. pressure.) Add remaining ingredients and heat through. Add 1 T. mild Picante sauce. Serve hot in chip lined bowls and top with chopped tomatoes, olives and grated cheese, if desired. Makes 3 1/2 cups.

Cal. 161 **Fat** .5g/3% **Carb.** 24g **Fbr.** 8g **Pro.** 17g

CREAMY SPROUT BALLS

1 c. ground nuts   *3 T. honey*
1/2 c. sunflower sprouts   *1/2 t. vanilla*
1/2 c. fat-free cream cheese or yogurt cream cheese

Mix, form into balls and chill. Can be rolled in toasted nuts, coconut, or granola. Makes 24 one inch balls.

To make Yogurt Cream Cheese, pour 1 qt. yogurt into a colander lined with 3 layers of cheesecloth or a 15" piece of cotton mesh fabric. Let drain 10 minutes, then gather edges of cloth and hang for 8-10 hours. Scrape cheese from bag and use or refrigerate. Whey (the water that drips from yogurt) can be used in soups or breads in place of water.

Cal. 65 Fat .7g/10% Carb. 13g Fbr. 1g Pro. 3g (per ball)

NUT AND RAISIN BALLS

1 c. raisins   *1 c. nuts*
1 c. sprouted wheat   *1/2 c. sunflower sprouts*

Mix and grind in blender or meat grinder. Form into balls or press into pan and cut into squares. Serve as is or add toasted coconut or granola. Makes 24 balls.

Cal. 81 **Fat** 5g/50% **Carb.** 9g **Fbr.** 1g **Pro.** 2g (per ball)

WHEAT AND NANAS

1 c. sprouted wheat   *2 sliced bananas*
1 c. shredded coconut

Slice bananas on an angle (Oriental style) and coat with mixed sprouts and coconut. Add toothpicks and serve. Serves 4-6.

Cal. 118 **Fat** 9g/35% **Carb.** 18g **Fbr.** 2g **Pro.** 2g

SPROUTS SUPREME

1 c. sprouted wheat   *1/4 c. sunflower sprouts*
2 c. dates or raisins   *1/4 c. honey*
1 c. nuts   *1/4 c. toasted coconut*

Finely grind sprouts, dates and nuts in meat grinder. Add honey and mix well. Form into balls or bars and coat with coconut. Chill. Makes 36 balls.

Cal. 73 **Fat** 3g/34% **Carb.** 11g **Fbr.** 1g **Pro.** 1g (per ball)

FROZEN BANANA HAYSTACKS

2 bananas   *1 c. 2-day wheat sprouts*
1/2 c. melted carob   *1 c. shredded coconut*

Slice bananas into 1/2" pieces. Place 1/2 t. melted carob on top. Dip in mixed sprouts and coconut. Freeze until firm. Serves 6-8.

These can also be topped with granola, rice crispies, or a combination of sprouts, coconut, and dry cereal. (Try mixing a few tablespoons of peanut butter with the melted carob.)

Cal. 167 **Fat** 8.5g/44% **Carb.** 21g **Fbr.** 3g **Pro.** 4g

PORCUPINE EGGS

1 c. 3-day wheat sprouts
1 c. raisins
1 t. vanilla

1/3 c. chunky peanut butter
1 c. coconut

Toast coconut, if desired. Reserve 1/2 to coat "eggs". Finely grind sprouts and raisins in a hand food grinder or electric food processor. Mix all ingredients and form into 24 balls. Roll in coconut and serve.

For an extra special treat, add 1/2 c. carob or butterscotch chips.

Cal. 60 **Fat** 3g/42% **Carb.** 8g **Fbr.** .8g **Pro.** 2g (per ball)

CAROB WHEAT SPROUT BALLS

2 c. 3-day wheat sprouts
1 c. peanut butter
1/4 c. carob powder
1 c. nuts or sunflower seeds

1 c. raisins
3 T. honey
Coconut to coat balls

Finely grind sprouts, raisins and nuts. Mix in honey and carob powder and form into 36 balls. Roll in toasted coconut. Eat within 1 day or sprouts tend to harden.

Cal. 100 **Fat** 6.3g/52% **Carb.** 10g **Fbr.** 1g **Pro.** 3g (per ball)

SPROUTED WHEAT SQUARES

1 c. 3-day sprouted wheat
1 c. dates
1/2 c. chunky peanut butter

1 c. toasted coconut
1/2 c. carob chips, melted
1 t. vanilla

Reserve 1/2 coconut. Mix peanut butter and melted carob chips. Finely grind sprouted wheat and dates. Add remaining ingredients and press into 8" square pan. Top with remaining coconut. Cut into squares and serve.

Cal. 102 **Fat** 5.4g/42% **Carb.** 12g **Fbr.** 1g **Pro.** 3g (per square)

Powdered Milk Cheeses

These cheeses are SO quick to make, they're almost instant. The taste and texture of powdered milk cheeses are slightly different than commercial cheeses, which makes them infinitely more versatile and definitely worth the small amount of time necessary to make them.

Milk in one form or another has been used in all recipes, adding a high-quality protein that is inexpensive and easy to store. For those who have a lot of dry milk on hand, I hope you will enjoy these FUN, FAST and DELICIOUS new ways to use powdered milk.

USES FOR HOMEMADE CHEESE AND COTTAGE CHEESE

UNFLAVORED CHEESES: Soups; salads; sandwiches; taco filling; stir-fry; omelets; patties; loaves; casseroles; lasagna; on freshly sliced tomatoes; or mixed with 1/2 commercial cottage or grated cheese.

FLAVORED CHEESES: Chip dips; sandwich fillings; casserole toppings; jerky; mixed with Parmesan to use on top of pizza and spaghetti; seasoned with Curry Powder to use in cracked wheat and rice Pilaf; and as "CHEESEBURGER."

INGREDIENTS USED IN THIS SECTION

DRY MILK POWDER - All recipes are written using non-instant milk, but any *powdered milk* will work. To reduce the volume of instant milks with large crystals (like the grocery store variety), place crystals in a dry blender and process to a fine powder. They can then be used in any recipe calling for "dry milk powder." Don't throw away "old milk." The cheese recipes in this book are the perfect way to use old, slightly off-flavor, stored-too-long milk powder. The rinsing and draining process washes away the yellow color and old flavor.

MILK CURDLERS - The following acids are used to curdle the milk: ascorbic acid powder, commonly called Vitamin C (found at drug stores, health food stores and pharmaceutical companies); citric acid (found at pharmacies, restaurant supplies, sometimes in grocery stores with pickling supplies); fresh or bottled lemon or lime juice; rennet tablets; yogurt; buttermilk; acidophilus (a culture much like buttermilk); and white vinegar. My favorites are rennet tablets, fresh lemon juice and white vinegar.

Freeze dried cultures of yogurt, buttermilk and acidophilus are used in some recipes and should be stored in the freezer for the time when we may not have fresh starts available.

OPTIONAL EQUIPMENT

Candy/Deep-Fry Thermometer: The metal type with a round register on top and a 6-8" metal post are available in most grocery stores for about $5.00. This would be helpful the first few times you try a different type of cheese.

Cloth for draining cheeses: Buy cotton cheesecloth (made for cheese) or other loose weave fabric. I prefer to use a fine cotton mesh t-shirt knit (purchased at a fabric store) because the fabric is sturdy enough to wash, sterilize by boiling and then use over and over again. If you use a fabric with a weave that is too fine, as in most fabrics, cheese will drain too slowly. I use a 22"x15" piece of fabric (longer on one end to allow for shrinkage with the long side being cut parallel to the selvage edge). A yard of fabric will be enough for 6 squares, which should be a year's supply. If you use cheesecloth, cut a 40" long piece of fabric (sold as a tube of fabric). Following the illustration below, turn one end of fabric over the rest (folding like a pair of socks) until ends meet and fabric forms a double tube. Secure edges with a rubber band and stretch open end over colander or strainer.

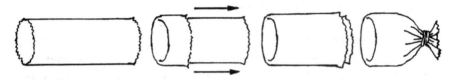

NON-FAT DRY MILK INFORMATION

NONFAT DRY MILK, usually non-instant, is a good source of protein. According to the Ezra Taft Benson Institute (Brigham Young University, Provo, UT, 84602), 50 pounds of dry milk powder would feed one person for one year. This amount would provide 22.2 grams of protein per day and could be consumed as three 8-oz. glasses of milk or 1/2 cup of cheese. (Having Your Food Storage and Eating It, Too, Benson Institute.)

The brand of non-instant milk I use requires 3 cups of dry powder to make 1 gallon of liquid milk. Adjust the recipes to the quantities given for your particular brand of powdered milk.

Reconstituted milk can be used in place of fresh milk in drinks, baked goods, puddings, or in any recipe you may already be using. However, in this volume, non-instant milk powder is used to make LIQUID MILK, BUTTERMILK, SOFT AND HARD CHEESES, YOGURT and YOGURT CHEESES, imitation SOUR CREAM, CREAM CHEESE and "CHEESEBURGER" (a meat-textured cheese).

Why fat-free cheeses do not melt

Most homemade skim milk cheeses have the unique quality of not melting, just like Tofu made from soybeans or Gluten made from wheat. These products are isolated proteins from those foods and are an excellent high quality protein addition to stir fry, soups, patties and casseroles, tossed or molded salads or as sandwich spreads. Yogurt can be used to make sour cream and cream cheese and makes a good slicing and melting cheese.

For a creamy, **meltable** cheese, oil can be added. If the cottage cheese recipe calls for 2 c. water + 1 1/2 c. dry milk powder, I add 1/3 c. oil, most of which will be washed out in the rinsing process.

What is a Direct-Acid Process?

Flavor-causing enzymes come from bacteria which produce acid and then release enzymes. That bacteria is found in commercial cheesemaking cultures, but since those cultures are expensive and have a very short shelf life, I eliminate the long culturing process and use an acid to curdle the milk while the milk is heating. This is a direct-acid method (meaning acid is added to the milk to eliminate the need to use cheese cultures which require hours of incubation time).

These cheeses have a different taste and texture than commercial cheeses. The resulting cheeses are flavored with buttermilk or other spices and herbs. When I want a different flavor or texture, or a cheese that can be aged for 1-2 months, I use buttermilk, yogurt or acidophilus as cultures.

Because of this direct acid process, nearly all cheeses in this volume can be made in 8 minutes or less, from start to finish. *Most cook in only 3 minutes!*

Can I reuse the whey?

Whey from the cheesemaking process can be used to replace water in nearly any recipe. It can also be used in place of water in the cheese recipes in this book. Whey can be reused up to 3 times in making cottage cheese, resulting in a sweeter cheese with each use. The sweet cheese can be made into sweet dips and sauces for crackers and fruit salads. (Note: If you are using old milk, you will get a stronger, less desirable flavor with each batch.)

What to do with OLD powdered milk

Do you have OLD, OLD milk, slightly yellowed, and so strong that no one will drink it? A hot water rinse takes away the old flavor and the yellow color. A second rinse, using cool water, firms the curds. Using this method, the resulting cheese tastes just as good as that made from fresh milk powder.

Curdling agents

ANY acid will curdle milk, but some **taste** better than others. Cheeses that are rinsed well will usually retain only a little of the flavor of the acid used as the curdling agent. The following is a list of my favorite acids for cheesemaking:

• **Fresh lemon juice** is my #1 all-time best acid for 3-minute cheeses, but I don't always keep lemons on hand. The after-taste is very pleasant, making this the perfect acid for firm cheeses that are not as well-rinsed as small-curd cheeses.

• **Reconstituted lemon juice** most often forms very tiny curds, perfect for parmesan cheese.

• **White vinegar** is the easiest acid to store, and the flavor washes away during rinsing. Makes a firm, solid curd, and a perfect meat substitute, "cheeseburger."

• **Rennet** is a traditional slow-acting curdling agent used in cheesemaking. Adding it in larger quantities than normal causes milk to "set" quickly. Rennet produces a soft, creamy cottage cheese. Also excellent for cream cheese, homemade ice cream, puddings and custards. Rennet is found in many grocery stores, in the "jello" aisle. If your store doesn't carry it, see p. 188 for ordering information. It stores well in the refrigerator or freezer, so keep a supply on hand.

• **Yogurt and Buttermilk** produce cheeses that taste more like the "real thing." However, they vary in strength, depending on manufacturer and age of the product, so it takes some experimenting to know how much to add to curdle your milk. They are best used to "sour" milk that will then curdle when heated without the addition of additional acid.

• **Vitamin C powder** (Ascorbic Acid) works very well, but loses potency after several months, so adjustments must be made in quantities used. Store in refrigerator for best results. Vitamin C tablets do not work well, as they contain fillers and binders that sometimes produce off-flavored and off-colored cheeses.

Can I make yellow cheeses?

Cheese colorings can be added to any recipe during the blending process. Dairies, some health food or preparedness stores and cheesemaking mail order catalogs carry liquid or tablet forms of yellow cheese coloring. Paste coloring can also be obtained from stores that carry cake decorating supplies. Ordinary food coloring for home use is not permanent and will not work, as it washes out during the rinsing process.

Important Hint to keep cheeses from sticking to the cooking pan:
Before adding milk to the pan, warm pan first, then spray the inside with cooking spray and reheat until spray turns slightly brown.

CHEESE RECIPES

Cottage cheese in 3 minutes? Firm curds (excellent for dips and sandwich spreads) can be made quickly and easily with a minimum of equipment. The best tasting soft curd cottage cheese is made with buttermilk added to the rinsed and salted curds to make it creamy and give it a slightly soured taste.

RENNET CHEESE

1 qt. hot tap water
2 junket rennet tablets
* dissolved in 1 T. cold water*

1 c. buttermilk
2 c. dry milk powder
2 T. vegetable oil (opt.)

Blend all ingredients and place in a heavy saucepan coated with a non-stick pan spray. Let sit undisturbed for 10 minutes. Cut or stir to break into curds and cook over medium heat for 5 minutes. Pour curds into a strainer, rinse with hot then cold water and drain. Salt to taste, then refrigerate. Or, place in a cheese-cloth bag and press as shown on page 10. This is a very mild cheese, good with salt and chopped chives. Use within 3-4 days.

To make cream cheese from this recipe, reduce rennet to 1/4 tablet and add 1 c. buttermilk when mixing ingredients. Set in a warm place overnight. After cutting set curds into cubes, place curds over medium heat and cook 5 minutes. Pour into a cheesecloth-lined colander and let rest 15 minutes. Gather edges of bag, secure with a rubber band and hang or press until firm like cream cheese.

Cal. 61 **Fat** .1g/2% **Carb.** 9g **Fbr.** 0g **Pro.** 6g

SOFT COTTAGE CHEESE

2 c. hot water
3 T. fresh lemon juice or white vinegar

1 1/2 c. dry milk powder

Blend water and dry milk and pour into saucepan (foam and all). Sprinkle lemon juice or vinegar slowly around edges and gently stir over medium heat just until milk begins to curdle, separating into curds and whey. Remove from heat and let rest 1 minute. Pour into a strainer or colander, rinse with hot then cold water. Press out water with back of spoon. Makes about 1 1/2 c. curds. If desired, moisten rinsed curds with a little buttermilk before serving and add salt to taste. Refrigerate if not used immediately. Whey from fresh milk powder can be used in place of water in breads and soups.

Cal. 47 **Fat** .1g/2% **Carb.** 7g **Fbr.** 0g **Pro.** 5g

QUICK SOFT PRESSED CHEESE

2 c. boiling water
3 T. vegetable oil
3-4 T. fresh lemon juice

1 1/2 c. dry milk powder
1 c. buttermilk
cheese coloring tablets (opt.)

Blend water, milk and oil, allowing foam to settle slightly. If colored cheese is desired, add 1/2 tablet cheese coloring (or cake decorating paste color) while blending. Pour into hot saucepan coated with a non-stick pan spray and heat to at least 160°F. Add lemon juice and continue to stir until mixture curdles.

Pour into a cheesecloth-lined colander. Rinse curds with warm water, then salt to taste. Place cheese in cloth between 2 plates or spoon into a cheese press. Apply weight and let sit for 1/2 hour or longer, depending on how firm you want the cheese to be. Remove from plates or cheese press, rinse, wrap in plastic and refrigerate. Use within 1 month or freeze. This cheese can be sliced, grated, or crumbled. For "Smoked" Cheese, add 1/2 t. Liquid Smoke flavoring and 1/2-1 t. salt after rinsing curds.

Cal. 81 **Fat** 2.4g/27% **Carb.** 9g **Fbr.** 0g **Pro.** 6g

**Please note: Reference will be made to these 2 methods of pressing cheeses throughout this book.

PARMESAN CHEESE

1 c. boiling water
2-3 T. reconstituted lemon juice

1 c. dry milk powder

Blend all ingredients and cook in saucepan, coated with a non-stick cooking spray, over medium-high heat until milk boils. The curds will be very small and milk will be frothy. Pour into a cloth lined strainer, rinse and press out excess water. Put curds into a bowl and stir with a fork to break up. Spread on a cookie sheet and dry for about 10 minutes in a 150 degree oven. This cheese can be salted and used in place of Parmesan, or mixed 1/4 to 1/2 dried Parmesan cheese. Refrigerate or freeze. Makes about 1 c. curds.

Cal. 21 **Fat** 0g/2% **Carb.** 9g **Fbr.** 0g **Pro.** 6g

QUESO BLANCO

A Latin American cheese with a bland flavor, this is excellent in soups, stir-fry, and as a substitute for tofu. It browns nicely and takes on the flavor of the spices in any recipe.

2 c. warm water
1/4 c. white vinegar

1 1/2 c. dry milk powder

Blend all ingredients. Spray a heavy saucepan with a non-stick pan spray. Heat to form a coating, then add milk mixture. Cook over medium heat, stirring until curds form and remaining liquid is a clear yellow. If still milky looking, add more vinegar, 1 t. at a time.

Pour curds into a strainer and rinse well with hot water to remove vinegar flavor. Add salt to taste and press if desired. See page 116.

Cheese can then be cut into thin strips, bite-size pieces or other shapes. Refrigerate, stored in plastic wrap or in a covered container for up to one week. Or, freeze for 2-3 months.

Cal. 62 **Fat** .1g/0% **Carb.** 10g **Fbr.** 0g **Pro.** 6g

BAG CHEESE

2 c. boiling water
2 T. vegetable oil

1 c. dry milk powder
3-4 T. fresh lemon juice or white vinegar

Blend water, oil and dry milk. In a heavy saucepan coated with a non-stick pan spray, bring mixture almost to a boil, add lemon juice and gently stir just until milk curdles, about 15 seconds. Pour into a cloth-lined strainer. Let drain 5 minutes. Gather edges of cloth and tie or secure with a rubber band. Squeeze out excess moisture or hang for 2-3 hours, until dripping stops. Makes about 1 1/2 c. cheese. Salt undrained curds, if desired. Can be sliced, crumbled or grated when chilled.

Cal. 88 **Fat** 2.8g/7% **Carb.** 2g **Fbr.** 0g **Pro.** 5g

WHITE CHEESE

2 qt. warm water
3 cups dry milk powder
3 T. vegetable oil
2 junket rennet tablets dissolved in 2 T. cold water

1 c. fresh buttermilk (or use
   freeze-dried buttermilk starter)

Mix buttermilk with water and dry milk powder and let stand 4-8 hours. Heat milk to 90°F and add dissolved rennet tablet, stirring for one minute, then let stand for one hour. Mixture will be set. Turn stove on lowest heat and gently stir curds until temperature reaches 102°F. Put pan in a sink filled with hot water and add additional boiling water as necessary to maintain temperature for 1 1/2 hours, stirring curds every 15 minutes. Let rest 1/2 hour.

Strain off whey, rinse, add 1 T. salt and stir well. Let rest 10 minutes and then place in cheese press or between plates. Press 4 hours. Remove from press and cut in quarters. Let stand 10 minutes to dry. Wrap in plastic, date and refrigerate for 1-2 months. This cheese is similar to commercial cheeses.

Cal. 59 **Fat** 1.7g/26% **Carb.** 7g **Fbr.** 0g **Pro.** 4g

MOCK MOZZARELLA

4 c. warm water
2 T. vegetable oil
2 junket rennet tablets dissolved in 1 T. cold water

3 c. dry milk powder
1 c. liquid buttermilk

Blend all ingredients, pour into saucepan coated with a non-stick pan spray and let sit, undisturbed, for 5 minutes. Cut curds into 1/2" cubes or stir to break up curds. Place pan over medium heat to firm curds. Pour curds and whey into a strainer; rinse with hot then cool water. Drain, then salt to taste. Place in cheesecloth bag and hang to drain, squeeze out excess liquid, or place in cheese press, as shown on page 116. Cool and grate or crumble. Use as you would commercial mozzarella.

Note: This has the texture and meltability of commercial cheese, but not quite the same flavor. You could mix 1 c. grated Mock Mozzarella with 1/2 c. commercial Mozzarella for an authentic flavor.

Cal. 94 **Fat** 3.5g/33% **Carb.** 10g **Fbr.** 0g **Pro.** 6g

YELLOW CHEDDAR CHEESE

4 c. lukewarm water   *3 c. dry milk powder*
2/3 c. vegetable oil*   *1 3/4 c. white vinegar*
6 T. cheddar cheese powder (or add 1 cheese coloring tablet to water)
*Note: Most of this oil is washed away in the rinsing process.

Blend all ingredients (except cheese powder, if used). Pour into hot saucepan coated with a non-stick pan spray and heat to 115°F to form curds. Rinse and drain curds in warm water and salt to taste. Add cheese powder, if used and mix well.

Put into cheese press or hang in cheesecloth bag and press out excess whey. After 15 minutes, remove from press or cloth, wrap in plastic, write date on package and refrigerate. Grate or slice as you would regular cheddar. If desired, grate and mix with 1/2 grated commercial cheddar.

Cal. 96 **Fat** 3.5g/32% **Carb.** 11g **Fbr.** 0g **Pro.** 6g

NO-COOK COTTAGE CHEESE

3 cups very warm water   *2 c. dry milk powder*
1 junket rennet tablet   *1 c. buttermilk*
    dissolved in 2 T. cold water

Mix or blend and pour into a quart container. Let stand in warm place 8-10 hours, until set and slightly soured. Stir with a fork to break into curds. Pour into a strainer and rinse gently in very hot water for about 2 minutes, then cold water for 1 minute. Drain for about 30 minutes and salt to taste.

For a firmer curd, use 2 rennet tablets and put blended ingredients into medium-sized bowl and let sit 20 minutes. Then cut or stir to break into small curds and drain in cheesecloth-lined colander. Cover drained curds with boiling water. Let stand 10 minutes. This can be used to replace cottage cheese in recipes, or can be pressed in a cheesecloth bag to make a delicious, mild cream cheese.

Cal. 81 **Fat** 2g/2% **Carb.** 12g **Fbr.** 0g **Pro.** 8g

PANIR

2 c. boiling water   *1 1/2 c. dry milk powder*
1 c. plain yogurt

Blend water and dry milk powder and bring mixture back to a boil in a saucepan coated with vegetable spray. Stir in yogurt and bring to a boil again. The milk will curdle. Pour curds into a strainer and rinse with warm then cold water. Drain, salt and refrigerate. For a more solid cheese, press overnight between two plates. The pressed curds can be sliced very thin, then cut into small squares and fried to a light golden brown color and added to salads, sandwich fillings, stir fry, curry dishes, soups and casseroles. Makes 2 cups.

Cal. 84 **Fat** 1.4g/15% **Carb.** 12g **Fbr.** 0g **Pro.** 8g

CARAWAY CHEESE

1 T. caraway seeds   *2 c. boiling water*

Boil seeds and water for 15 minutes. Strain liquid and use to replace water in recipes for Panir or Soft cottage cheese, adding additional water if necessary. When curds are drained and rinsed, add caraway seeds and salt to taste. Press, if desired.

Cal. 85 **Fat** 1.4g/14% **Carb.** 13g **Fbr.** 0g **Pro.** 8g

JALAPENO CHEESE

Follow instructions for Caraway Cheese, substituting *1 T. chopped jalapeno peppers* for caraway seeds.

Cal. 85 **Fat** 1.4g/14% **Carb.** 13g **Fbr.** 0g **Pro.** 8g

"CHEESEBURGER"

"Cheeseburger" is a fast, versatile, delicious substitute for meat, tofu, or gluten and an especially good way to add complete protein to meals while using up all that old powdered milk so many people have on hand.

"Cheeseburger" can be used in any recipe calling for hamburger pieces, meat strips or chunks and can be refrigerated, frozen, bottled or dried. Fresh, refrigerated curd can be stored in or out of water for at least 2 weeks and can be bottled like any fresh meat. Frozen curd will last up to 6 months, depending on how it is wrapped or otherwise protected from freezer burn.

In its dried form, "Cheeseburger" can be kept without refrigeration, under sterile conditions, for at least 3 months. Dried and bottled, it should last indefinitely, as does textured vegetable protein (TVP), which is made from soybeans.

"CHEESEBURGER"

Place well drained Queso Blanco curds (press out excess liquid), in a bowl and add the following:

1-2 t. beef-flavored bouillon   *1 T. soy sauce*
a few drops liquid smoke (to taste)

Stir in flavorings, then granules are ready to use! Add to casseroles, loaves, patties, etc., or mix with cooked hamburger. Can be frozen.

Cal. 85 **Fat** 1.4g/14% **Carb.** 13g **Fbr.** 0g **Pro.** 8g

OR, make a double or triple batch and use one of the following methods, all of which can be frozen:

Fried: Fry well drained curds in a small amount of oil or butter until lightly browned, like hamburger granules. Try making a large batch to keep on hand for a week's worth of meals.

Dried: Dry in dehydrator or on baking sheet coated with vegetable spray, until firm for refrigerator storage, or brittle for long-term storage.

"CHEESEBURGER" STRIPS OR PIECES - Press an entire batch of seasoned or plain Queso Blanco curd overnight. Cut into strips or bite-sized pieces and process using any of the above methods for curds.

LONG TERM STORAGE OF "CHEESEBURGER"

Drying: Curds can be slowly dried on an ungreased baking sheet in a 150°F oven with the door slightly ajar until hard and tough. Store in glass jar with a sealing lid. If you made curds in quantity, fill pint or quart jars with warm curds. Put rings and heated lids on jars and return to 150°F oven for 25 minutes (or boiling water bath for 30 minutes). Remove and cool. Jars will seal because of the heat, but may not form a vacuum. Store in cool room up to 1 year.

To rehydrate: Add flavored granules to soups about 5 minutes before serving, just enough time to soften, but not so long that they lose their flavor. If the granules or strips are unflavored, add at the beginning of the cooking time so they can absorb flavors.

"CHEESEBURGER PATTIES"

4 c. warm water   *4 c. dry milk powder*
1/2+ c. white vinegar

Put 2 c. water in hot saucepan coated with vegetable spray, and bring to a boil. Place remaining water and dry milk powder to blender. Blend and pour into boiling water. Over medium heat, stir and slowly add vinegar until milk curdles. Do not boil.

Pour into colander and rinse in hot water. Add vegetable- or meat-based seasoning (chicken, beef, ham, vegetable) of your choice, if desired. Shape into six 3" patties. Place 3 on each plate; stack and press liquid out with hands for about 1 minute, allowing liquid to drain off. Steam or pan-fry. If desired, coat with egg and breading before frying.

Cal. 55 **Fat** .1g/2% **Carb.** 19g **Fbr.** 0g **Pro.** 5g

BARBECUE "CHEESEBURGER" PATTIES

Follow above recipe for patties, but add the following to hot curds before forming and pressing:

1 c. finely diced onion
2 t. barbecue seasoning (dry)

1 t. dried parsley

Add patties (or cut into strips) one layer at a time to the following simmering broth in a 4 quart saucepan. Cook for 30 seconds before adding second layer. Simmer patties for 10 minutes.

Broth:

3 c. water
1 t. liquid smoke
2 t. Kitchen Bouquet (opt) for dark brown color

2 T. beef-flavored bouillon
1 t. soy sauce

Makes 6 to 8 3" patties. Note: For Oriental Cheeseburger Patties, substitute 1 t. powdered ginger or powdered sweet & sour seasoning.

Cal. 178 Fat .6g/3% Carb. 20g Fbr. 0g Pro. 12g

CHICKEN "CHEESEBURGER" PIECES

1 recipe Queso Blanco
2 c. boiling water
1/4 t. black pepper

1 t. parsley
2 T. chicken-flavored bouillon
1 t. soy sauce

After rinsing Queso Blanco curds in hot water, form a ball with hands and squeeze out any excess liquid. Using a fork, "peel" bite-sized chunks of cheese from the ball to resemble chicken chunks. Heat remaining ingredients and drop in cheese pieces. Do not boil. Cook for15 minutes, then drain and use as chicken pieces in any recipe.

Cal. 68 Fat .2g/3% Carb. 16g Fbr. 0g Pro. 8g

"CHEESEBURGER" SAUSAGE

2 c. crumbled Queso Blanco
2 eggs or 4 egg whites
2 T. oil

1 t. soy sauce
2-4 T. white bean or wheat flour
1-2 T. sausage seasoning*

Mix all ingredients well, adding only enough flour to make a stiff dough. Shape in patties or sausage shapes. Put into oiled skillet and brown on all sides. OR, add only 1 egg and stir fry as small chunks, like hamburger. Makes 2 1/2 cups. Use for pizzas, salads, with scrambled eggs, or in casseroles.

*Pork Sausage Seasoning is carried or can be ordered at many grocery stores. OR, use the following recipe to make your own seasoning mix.

Cal. 78 **Fat** .9g/10% **Carb.** 14g **Fbr.** 0g **Pro.** 9g

SAUSAGE SEASONING

1 1/2 T. ground rosemary
3 1/2 T. salt
5 t. ground basil
1 T. cayenne pepper

5 T. ground sage
5 t. ground marjoram
4 t. garlic powder
1/2 t. black pepper

Mix ingredients well. Store in jar. Label. Shake before using. Makes 1/2 cup. (The Amazing Wheat Book, by LeArta Moulton. Used by Permission)

BREADED CHICKEN TENDERS

1 recipe Cheeseburger Patties, p. 126
1 c. corn flake crumbs
1/4 c. white bean flour
1/3 c. warm water

1/8 t. pepper
1/2 t. chicken-flavored bouillon
1/8 t. poultry seasoning
1/8 t. rosemary

Shape patties into thin patties or chicken breast shapes. Make a batter from bean flour, water and seasonings. Dip patties in batter, then in crumbs. Pan-fry in pan-sprayed or buttered skillet until brown on both sides. Serve hot or cold, with gravy, on a sandwich, or in a salad.

Cal. 97 **Fat** .2g/2% **Carb.** 8g **Fbr.** 0g **Pro.** 11g

FISH STICKS OR STEAKS

1 recipe Cheeseburger Patties, p. 126　　*2 t. clam base or 1/2 c. tuna juice*
2 c. hot water　　　　　　　　　　　　*up to 1/3 c. warm water*
1 T. clam base or 1/4 c. tuna juice　　*1/4 c. white bean flour*
　　　　　　　　　　　　　　　　　　1 c. cracker or bread crumbs

Season warm rinsed curds with 1 T. clam base or tuna juice. Work quickly, as cooled curds will not hold together. Shape into squares or strips. Dip into batter made from clam base, water and bean flour, then in crumbs. Coat skillet with baking spray and brown on both sides. Serve hot or cold. Great for sandwiches or salads. Can be topped with tartar sauce.

Cal. 169 **Fat** 1.4g/8% **Carb.** 14g **Fbr.** 0g **Pro.** 11g

"CLAMBURGER" OR MOCK CRAB

2 c. Queso Blanco cheese　　　　　　*1 T. clam bouillon or soup base*
1 c. tuna juice from water-pack tuna　*3 c. water*
　(I save drained juice in freezer.)

Drop cut and pressed, clam-sized pieces of cheese into boiling tuna juice, water and bouillon. Cover and cook 15 minutes over low heat. (Pressure cooking for 15 minutes at 15 lb. pressure produces tougher pieces with a more clam-like texture.) Use in soups, casseroles, omelets, quiche. Makes 2 cups.

Mock Crab can be made using this recipe, substituting crab soup base for the clam base.

Cal. 70 **Fat** .2g/2% **Carb.** 13g **Fbr.** 0g **Pro.** 13g

SOURED MILK PRODUCTS

Homemade sour cream or cream cheese from powdered milk can be used in any of your favorite recipes calling for commercial products (and at a fraction of the cost). If you have the "real thing" available, try mixing equal portions of a commercial product with your homemade powdered milk product. You'll never know the difference!

Remember, heating yogurt and sour cream or adding sour milk to hot liquids can result in curdling, so use caution. Always add a little of the hot mixture to the sour milk product at a time or heating mixture in the top of a double boiler, unless otherwise directed.

THE FOLLOWING CHANGES OCCUR DURING THE FERMENTING PROCESS:

- During the culturing (souring) process, milk protein becomes easier to digest.

- Lactose is converted to lactic acid, which aids in digestion and in assimilating protein, calcium and iron.

- Alcohol and carbonic acid are produced which soothe the nerves of the intestinal tract.

- It appears that vitamin B, folic and folinic acids are synthesized, making them easier for our bodies to use.

CULTURED BUTTERMILK is made by souring reconstituted milk with a small amount of fresh or freeze dried buttermilk starter. This starter introduces a large number of active milk-souring bacteria which play a vital role in preventing the development of other bacteria that might give the milk undesirable flavors and odors. Buttermilk is used to add flavor and organisms, as well as acidity to various cheeses.

HOMEMADE BUTTERMILK

1 qt. lukewarm water   *1 c. dry milk powder*
1/2 c. buttermilk, commercial or homemade

Stir well and cover. Let stand in a warm place (at least 80°F) until clabbered, about 12-18 hours. Stir until smooth. Refrigerate. To keep the buttermilk fresh, a new batch should be made every two weeks. Older buttermilk that is still free from mold may not work well as a starter culture, but will still be effective in curdling cheeses. Makes 5 1/2 cups.

To use a freeze-dried buttermilk culture, make buttermilk according to package directions, then use the above recipe to make additional batches, just as you would use a sourdough start.

Cal. 37 **Fat** .2g/5% **Carb.** 7g **Fbr.** 0g **Pro.** 5g

BUTTERMILK SOUR CREAM

2 c. light cream   *2 T. buttermilk*

Shake or blend a few seconds. Cover the jar and let stand at 80°F for 24 hours. Refrigerate to set. Use in any recipe calling for sour cream.

Cal. 30 **Fat** 7.9g/86% **Carb.** .6g **Fbr.** 0g **Pro.** 4g

BUTTERMILK CHEESE

1 qt. homemade buttermilk   *1 1/2 c. dry milk powder*

Blend buttermilk and powder together and pour into a hot, heavy saucepan coated with a lecithin spray. Cook and stir over medium heat until milk begins to curdle. Let rest 5 minutes. If liquid is clear, pour curds into colander and drain off whey. If liquid is still milky, continue heating until liquid turns clear. Rinse in very warm, then cool water, salt and refrigerate. Note: Plain buttermilk without the added milk powder makes TINY curds and very small yield. Makes 1 1/2 cups.

Cal. 82 **Fat** .3g/3% **Carb.** 17g **Fbr.** 0g **Pro.** 12g

ACIDOPHILUS

ACIDOPHILUS is one form of bacteria used in making yogurt and can be obtained from health food stores in the form of fresh milk or freeze-dried grains). The culture is added to 90°F fresh or reconstituted dry milk in a glass container and incubated like yogurt at 80-90°F for 8-12 hours. The more grains of acidophilus present in the milk, the faster the milk will thicken. Some cultures will set firm like yogurt.

Note: To make 1 quart of acidophilus milk, I add 2 capsules to 3 3/4 c. warm water and blend in 1 1/2 c. dry milk powder.

ACIDOPHILUS CHEESE

1 qt. acidophilus milk   *1 1/2 c. dry milk powder*

Blend milk made from starter and dry milk powder together and pour into a hot, heavy saucepan coated with a vegetable spray. Heat, without stirring, over low heat to 110°F. A solid curd will form. Cut or break curd and continue heating to 130°F for firm curds. (Lower temperatures would make a nice cream cheese and higher temperatures would make hard curds which would have a more meat-like texture.) Pour curds into a strainer and drain off whey. Rinse in hot, then cold water, salt and refrigerate. Makes about 2 cups of wonderfully tart cheese.

Cal. 95 **Fat** 1.2g/11% **Carb.** 16g **Fbr.** 0g **Pro.** 12g

YOGURT

Yogurt, like the milk from which it is made, is a good source of calcium, riboflavin and protein. However, yogurt and other fermented milks develop somewhat different food values than are present in regular milk.

Additional health values include: "bactericidal powers against pathogens, ability to alleviate many gastrointestinal distresses and other disorders, usefulness in relieving antibiotic-induced effects and a beneficial role in lactose intolerance." (Yogurt, Kefir & Other Milk Cultures, Beatrice Trum Hunter.) (In easy to understand terms, that means an increased ability to fend off illness and disease, fewer upset stomachs and relief from some side effects of antibiotics. Often, yogurt can be used by those who have an allergy or intolerance to regular milk.)

Freeze dried yogurt and acidophilus cultures purchased from health food stores can be frozen for long-term storage. Yogurt made from a freeze-dried start can be used to start subsequent batches and could be kept going indefinitely, just like a sourdough start. The shelf life (unrefrigerated) of freeze dried yogurt or acidophilus starter is about 6 months. I used one powdered yogurt starter culture that was 2 years old (stored in a hot, humid trailer) which took 2 days to set, but subsequent batches made from the yogurt took only 4-5 hours to set. The bacteria present were most likely few in number, thus accounting for the necessity of a long incubation time. Store yogurt in the refrigerator at 35-45°F. The fresher the yogurt, the higher its bactericidal value (more abundant "friendly" bacteria).

Yogurt and acidophilus cheeses are the EASIEST to make. They do not require additional acid and can be made into very soft, creamy cheeses or hard cheeses.

WAYS TO INCUBATE YOGURT
- in quart jars on a heating pad set on medium and covered with a folded towel. Cover jars with another folded towel.
- in a wide mouth half-gallon or gallon thermos
- in quart jars set in an ice chest surrounded by 2-3" of hot water. Re-heat water as necessary to keep yogurt warm at least 4-6 hours.
- wrapped in a sleeping bag or heavy blankets
- in a bowl of water set over the pilot light of a gas stove, using a towel to cover both containers and keep in the heat
- in an oven heated to 100°F, then turned off and pilot light or oven light on
- any method that provides a constant temperature of 106 to 115°F for 4-6 hr.

WHAT WENT WRONG?

WATERY YOGURT - The protein in milk is denatured (changed) when heated to 180°F. This denaturing process makes the protein molecules hold on to more water, making a firm, creamy yogurt that will not separate easily. Yogurt made without using this heating process separates easily to water (whey), but will still produce a usable product. When making cheese from this yogurt, there will be fewer curds.

If you have a thermometer, make sure the milk is heated to at least 180°F, then cooled to 110°F before the yogurt culture is added, as the "friendly" bacteria in yogurt are destroyed at any temperature over 120°F. Once you get used to feeling how hot the milk should be at each stage, a thermometer will not be necessary.

YOGURT DOES NOT SET - If milk is still liquid after 4-5 hours, it may be because the fresh yogurt starter culture was too old (up to one week old is best) or the culture did not stay warm long enough. Allow mixture to incubate up to an additional 4 hours, testing every hour. If milk is still not set, refrigerate and use in place of milk in breads, pancakes, or any of the cheeses.

YOGURT BY THE GALLON

6 c. warm water
2 1/2 qt. lukewarm water

4 c. dry milk powder
2 capsules freeze-dried acidophilus
1/2 c. plain yogurt

Spray large saucepan with non-stick pan spray. Blend dry milk powder and *warm water* in two batches (3 c. of water at a time, using blender, egg beater or wire whip), then heat to 180°F, stirring constantly. Pour into a 1 gallon container. Add remaining water to milk mixture. Temperature should not be hotter than 110°F. If mixture is too hot, add cold water or ice cubes. Add opened acidophilus capsules and stirred yogurt. Mix well. Pour into quart jars and keep in a warm place where it will not be jiggled or moved. Choose one of the methods below for incubating.

- Put a heating pad on a countertop and set to medium. Place folded bath towel on top. Place quart jars on towel and cover with another towel, tucking in edges to form a warm "nest."
- Put quart jars in a large bowl of hot water and cover with a bath towel. After about 2 hours, add boiling water to reheat cooled water.
- Put quart jars in oven that has been heated to 100°F, then oven turned off and pilot lot or oven light on.

After 4-6 hours, the mixture should be set. Test with a spoon, rather than jiggling. Set yogurt should be refrigerated in the jars. This recipe will set up more firmly as the yogurt cools.

Use yogurt in fruit "shakes," on granola, in any bread recipe calling for milk, in individual bowls with frozen orange juice concentrate or honey jam stirred in, or to make yogurt cheeses. Makes 1 gallon.

Cal. 33 **Fat** .4g/2% **Carb.** 5g **Fbr.** 0g **Pro.** 3g

VANILLA YOGURT

3 3/4 qt. warm water
1 c. plain yogurt
1 T. vanilla

4 c. dry milk powder
3 T. unsweetened gelatin
1 c. melted honey

Soften gelatin in 1/4 c. cold water. Heat slightly to melt. Blend all ingredients well and pour into a 4 quart jars. Using one of the incubation methods above, place where it will stay warm and will not be disturbed. After 4-6 hours, yogurt should be "set." If mixture is still liquid, wait 1-2 more hours. When slightly firm, refrigerate. Serve plain or use in fruit "shakes," on granola, or in individual bowls with frozen juice concentrate or jam.

Cal. 73 **Fat** .3g/4% **Carb.** 14g **Fbr.** 0g **Pro.** 5g

YOGURT SOUR CREAM (UNCOOKED)

1 qt. yogurt   1/8 t. salt

Line a colander or large sieve with muslin, or other loose-weave fabric. Pour yogurt into colander. Cover and place in a bowl. Refrigerate to drain for 4 to 6 hours until consistency is like thick sour cream. With a spoon, scrape yogurt from fabric and place in a container; sprinkle with salt. Mix well. Store, covered, in refrigerator up to 3 weeks. American Dairy Association

Cal. 35 **Fat** .9g/0% **Carb.** 8g **Fbr.** 0g **Pro.** 2g

FAST YOGURT SOUR CREAM (COOKED)

1 qt. yogurt   1/8 t. salt
low-fat buttermilk or fat-free mayonnaise to moisten

Pour yogurt into a heavy saucepan over medium heat. Raise temperature to 110°F. Curds will start to separate from whey. Remove from heat and stir gently, then let rest 3 minutes. Pour into colander or large sieve lined with several layers of cheesecloth or other loose-weave fabric. Press out excess water with a spoon. Put into a small container and mix in buttermilk or fat-free mayonnaise and salt, if desired. Refrigerate for up to 2 weeks.

Cal. 35 **Fat** .9g/0% **Carb.** 8g **Fbr.** 0g **Pro.** 2g

YOGURT CREAM CHEESE (UNCOOKED)

1 qt. yogurt   *1/8 t. salt*

Line a colander or large sieve with muslin, other loose weave fabric or 4 layers of paper towels. Pour yogurt into colander. Cover and place in a bowl to drain. Refrigerate 8 to 10 hours. Remove from fabric or towels and place in a container; sprinkle with salt. Mix well. Store, covered, in refrigerator up to 3 weeks. American Dairy Association

Cal. 35 **Fat** .9g/0% **Carb.** 8g **Fbr.** 0g **Pro.** 2g

FAST YOGURT CREAM CHEESE (COOKED)

1 qt. yogurt   *1/8 t. salt*

Put yogurt into a heavy saucepan. Slowly heat to 115°F without stirring over low heat (about 15 minutes). Yogurt will have separated into very soft curds and whey. Stir slightly. Remove from heat and let rest 1 minute. Pour into a fine mesh strainer or loose weave cloth. Drain in strainer or hang in cloth until no whey drips (about 10 minutes). Add salt, stir and refrigerate in a covered container. For a more firm cheese, drain longer or pour into loose weave cloth, gather ends of cloth, twist, then press between two plates**, adding weight just until cheese starts to squeeze through bag. Press 1-2 hours. Drain off excess whey and refrigerate. Can be stored, covered, in refrigerator up to 3 weeks. Makes about 1 cup cheese.

This cheese can be flavored with caraway, garlic, dried Parmesan, olives, chives, green chilies, chili powder, pineapple, coconut, honey, or any other flavor you might see in commercial cream cheeses. See p. 160 for FLAVORED CREAM CHEESES.

****(Four Stars!) Meltable, spreadable and verrry edible! To melt cream cheese on top of meat or wheat patties, place a slice of firm, flavored cream cheese on oiled skillet and top with an already browned meat or vegetable patty. Fry 30 seconds to melt cheese, then remove from pan and serve.

Cal. 35 **Fat** .9g/0% **Carb.** 8g **Fbr.** 0g **Pro.** 2g

YOGURT COTTAGE CHEESE - FIRM CURD

1 qt. yogurt   *salt to taste*

Put yogurt into heavy saucepan and cook over medium heat to 130°F while stirring. Curd size will depend on how vigorously you stir. Pour into a strainer, rinse and salt to taste.

Soft curd - For softer curds, raise temperature to 115°F without stirring, then stir only enough to break up mass. Continue heating without stirring to 120°F. Pour into a strainer, rinse and salt to taste. Makes about 1 c. curds.

Cal. 35 **Fat** .9g/0% **Carb.** 8g **Fbr.** 0g **Pro.** 2g

MISCELLANEOUS MILK RECIPES

TO CREAM SOUPS:

To cream 2 quarts of soup, blend and heat:
1/2 cup white bean flour or cornstarch   2/3 c. dry milk powder

Cook 2-3 minutes and gradually stir in 4 cups of soup or broth until smooth. Slowly add this sauce to the hot soup, stirring until soup is creamy.

Cal. 47 **Fat** .01g/2% **Carb.** 8g **Fbr.** 1g **Pro.** 4g

"EVAPORATED" MILK SUBSTITUTE

1 c. hot water   *1/2 c. dry milk powder*
1/2 t. oil (optional)   *1 /4 t. honey*

Blend all ingredients well. If thicker milk is desired, add 1 1/2 t. tapioca starch and blend an additional 30 seconds. Makes 1 1/3 cups. Note: Keeps up to 1 week under refrigeration.

Cal. 18 **Fat** .3g/15% **Carb.** 2g **Fbr.** 0g **Pro.** 1g

BREAKFASTS

Start the day off right with a stick-to-the-ribs meal!

Lately, just the mention of eggs and cheese stirs up visions of excess fat and cholesterol sure to cause clogged arteries.

Using egg whites and fat-free cheeses eliminates the fat and cholesterol. The nonfat milk used in these recipes adds protein and calcium but not cholesterol, which is found in the fat of dairy products and meats.

In addition, recent research indicates that including whole grains in any diet will help to REDUCE cholesterol levels. Add whole grains and other high-fiber foods to your favorite breakfast recipes to help increase nutrition as well as fiber.

TIERED OMELET RANCHEROS

12 egg whites or 6 eggs
2 T. milk
3/4 t. salt
1/8 t. pepper
_____

2 c. canned tomatoes
1/8 t. salt
1/8 t. hot pepper sauce

1 4 oz. can green chilies, diced
2 c. cooked brown rice
1 T. cornstarch
1 T. cold water
1/2 c. yogurt
1 lg. avocado, diced
1 1/2 c. fat-free cottage cheese
1 c. grated cheese for garnish (opt.)

Beat eggs, milk, salt and pepper. Pour scant 1/2 c. egg mixture into skillet coated with vegetable spray. Tilt to spread. As mixture sets, lift at edges and let uncooked egg flow underneath. Brown on bottom. Invert on wax paper.

In saucepan, combine tomatoes, green chilies, rice, salt and hot sauce. Add cornstarch mixed with cold water. Heat and stir until thickened.

On a large, ovenproof glass or metal platter, place one omelet, spread with 1/2 of tomato mixture. On second omelet, spread yogurt and avocado pieces sprinkled with lemon juice. Top with another omelet. Spread with cottage cheese, then add remaining omelet. Cover with foil and bake at 350°F for 25 minutes. Uncover and top with remaining sauce and grated cheese, if used. Bake 5 minutes more. Slice into wedges and serve hot. Serves 6.

Cal. 209 **Fat** 4.6g/19% **Carb.** 25g **Fbr.** 2g **Pro.** 18g

"CHEESY" EGGS AND TOAST

6 slices whole wheat bread
1 c. fat-free cottage cheese
1 c. cooked brown rice
1/4 c. dry milk powder

6 egg whites
2 T. diced onion
1 c. warm water
1 T. Picante Sauce
1 t. dried parsley

Cube or tear bread into chunks and put into custard cups or muffin tins coated with vegetable spray. Spoon 2 T. cottage cheese and brown rice on top of each cup. Blend remaining ingredients (add salt and pepper if desired) and pour over bread. Bake at 350°F until set, about 20 min.

Cal. 126 **Fat** 1.8g/13% **Carb.** 5g **Fbr.** 0g **Pro.** 12g

BREAKFAST DRINKS

CAROB SYRUP

1/4 c. carob powder | 2/3 c. water
1/3 c. honey | 2 t. vanilla
2/3 c. dry milk powder or substitute | pinch of salt if desired

In a small saucepan, add carob powder and powdered milk to honey and mix well, then add water. Bring this blend almost to a boil and simmer 5 minutes, stirring frequently. Add vanilla and pour into small container. Store in fridge (1-2 months) and use as syrup for sundaes, or for carob milk.

Cal. 86 **Fat** .3g/3% **Carb.** 17g **Fbr.** 1g **Pro.** 3g

CAROB MILK

2 c. water, milk or substitute | 1/3 to 1/2 c. carob syrup

Put water and Carob Syrup in a glass. Stir well. Carob tends to settle to the bottom, so it may need stirring now and then as you drink. For frosty milk, add only 1 1/2 c. water and 6 ice cubes. For hot milk, add syrup to hot water and stir well. Serves 2.

Cal. 86 **Fat** .3g/3% **Carb.** 17g **Fbr.** 1g **Pro.** 3g

CAROB A L'ORANGE

2 c. ice cold water | 2 T. malted milk powder
1/4 t. orange extract | 2 T. honey
2 t. vanilla | 2/3 c. dry milk powder
1/8 t. cinnamon | 2 T. carob powder

Blend all ingredients until thoroughly mixed. Add 4-6 ice cubes, if desired. Serves 2.

Cal. 238 **Fat** 2.3g/8% **Carb.** 46g **Fbr.** 2g **Pro.** 11g

CAROB MINT AU LAIT

2 c. ice cold water
1/4 t. peppermint extract
1/2 t. vanilla
1/8 t. cinnamon

2 T. malted milk powder
2 T. honey
2/3 c. dry milk powder
2 T. carob powder

Blend, shake or still all ingredients until creamy. Add 4-6 ice cubes, if desired. Serves 2.

Cal. 235 **Fat** 2.3g/8% **Carb.** 46g **Fbr.** 2g **Pro.** 11g

CAROB MINT TEA

2 c. boiling water
2 t. dried mint leaves
1 T. powdered carob or 2 T. carob syrup

1 T. honey
1/3 d. dry milk powder

Add leaves to boiling water. Cover, remove from heat and steep 15 minutes. Strain and add honey, milk and carob. Stir well. Good hot or chilled. Try adding 4 ice cubes and blending until frothy.

Cal. 81 **Fat** .5g/5% **Carb.** 16g **Fbr.** 9g **Pro.** 5g

ORANGE JULIUS

1 egg
2 T. dry milk powder
1/4 c. honey

4 c. orange juice
1 tray ice cubes
1 T. vanilla

Blend egg, honey and dry milk, then add remaining ingredients and blend until smooth and frothy. Serves 2.

Cal. 206 **Fat** 1.8g/8% **Carb.** 44g **Fbr.** .5g **Pro.** 4g

HAWAIIAN SUNRISE

1 1/4 c. water	*4 T. dry milk powder*
1/3 c. pineapple juice concentrate	*1/2 t. vitamin C. powder*
1/2 t. coconut extract	*1 large frozen banana*
2 t. flaxseed oil	*10 small ice cubes*

This smoothie is packed with vitamin C, and the addition of flaxseed oil makes it a perfectly filling breakfast. Mix or blend until smooth. If desired, add 1/4 c. orange juice concentrate. Serves 2.

Cal. 117 **Fat.** .1/1% **Carb.** 27g **Fbr.** 0g **Pro.** 3g

WHITE GRAPE FREEZE

1 c. water	*1/3 c. dry milk powder*
1/2 t. vanilla	*1 c. frozen peach chunks*
1 frozen banana	*10 small ice cubes*
1/2 c. White Grape Juice concentrate	

Blend all ingredients until smooth. Serves 2.

Cal. 175 **Fat.** .5/2% **Carb.** 39g **Fbr.** 2g **Pro.** 6g

PEACHY COOL-ER

2 peaches, canned or bottled	*1/2 c. plain yogurt*
1/2 c. liquid from peaches	

Blend all ingredients until smooth. Serves 2.

Cal. 72 **Fat.** .1/1% **Carb.** 12g **Fbr.** 2g **Pro.** 3g

PINEAPPLE-ORANGE FRUIT CUBES

4 c. pineapple juice
1/8 t. coconut flavoring
12 oz. orange juice concentrate

4 c. yogurt
1 T. vanilla
1 c. dry milk powder

Blend all ingredients about 2 minutes in blender. Serve immediately or pour into 9 x 13 inch baking dish and freeze until firm. When ready to serve, cut into chunks and blend, adding water, milk or fruit juice to make a thick, creamy shake. Serves 8.

Cal. 123 **Fat** .2g/1.5% **Carb.** 26g **Fbr.** .2g **Pro.** 5g

CREAMY APRICOT DELIGHT

1 c. apricot nectar
3 T. honey or to taste
1 t. vanilla
1 egg

1/2 c. pineapple juice
1/4 c. dry milk powder
1 frozen banana (opt.)

Blend all ingredients until smooth and creamy. Serves 2.

Cal. 241 **Fat** .6g/2% **Carb.** 53g **Fbr.** 3g **Pro.** 8g

BANANA MILK

2 c. water or juice
2 ripe bananas
1 t. vanilla

1/4 c. dry milk powder
dash nutmeg
1/2 c. yogurt

Blend until smooth. Chill or substitute 6 ice cubes for 1/2 c. of the water or juice while blending. Serves 4.

Cal. 198 **Fat** .3g/2% **Carb.** 43g **Fbr.** 2g **Pro.** 4g

ORANGE ICEE

1/2 c. dry milk powder
2 t. vanilla
1 c. yogurt or buttermilk

2 t. lemon juice
3/4 c. frozen orange juice concentrate
3/4 c. frozen apple juice concentrate
1-2 trays ice cubes

Blend all ingredients, adding as much ice as your blender can handle. Mixture should be thick and ice well blended. Serves 4.

Cal. 240 **Fat** .4g/2% **Carb.** 50g **Fbr.** .6g **Pro.** 7g

ORANGE-APRICOT DELIGHT

3/4 c. frozen orange juice concentrate
3 T. lemon juice
1/2 c. apricot puree
1/2 c. dry milk powder

1/2 c. yogurt or buttermilk
2 t. vanilla
2 c. cracked ice
1 c. water

Blend on high speed until smooth and frothy. Serves 4.

Cal. 190 **Fat** .2g/1% **Carb.** 44g **Fbr.** 2g **Pro.** 6g

HI-PROTEIN FRUITSHAKE

2 frozen bananas
1 t. vanilla
1/8 t. nutmeg
1 c. yogurt or buttermilk
1 1/2 c. frozen apple juice concentrate

1 t. sesame seeds
1 T. raw sunflower seeds
1/8 t. cinnamon
2 c. water

Blend seeds and water well. Strain out hulls, if desired. Add remaining ingredients and blend until smooth and creamy. Serves 2.

*Note: Don't let the calories and fat scare you. This drink is power-packed with nutritious energy from whole, raw seeds and fresh fruits.

Cal. 474 **Fat** 19g/35% **Carb.** 66g **Fbr.** 0g **Pro.** 12g

SOUPS

Soups and stews are an important part of our menu all year. Hearty soups are especially nice one-pot meals, when served with fresh sprouts or a salad. A variety of fresh vegetables or specialty pasta can be added to "dress up" basic soups.

Try making a double or triple batch of soup and freezing what you do not use in plastic containers or ziploc bags. Simply thaw during the day (or more quickly in hot water or the microwave), then heat and serve.

For Faster Cooking: Grated vegetables and thin, diagonally sliced vegetables cook much faster than regular slices. Partially cooked beans and vegetables can be puréed to finish cooking more quickly. Beans, grains and legumes can be coarsely cracked in a blender or hand grain grinder. This cuts the cooking time down to less than half of normal. Stored in the freezer, cooked grains and beans can be added to any soup for added flavor, fiber and nutrition.

Soups keep well in the refrigerator, usually up to 10 days. You can change the looks of leftovers by making the original recipe into a cream soup. See recipe on page 137.

CREAMY CHICKEN 'N NOODLE SOUP

2 qt. boiling water
1/2 c. chopped onion
4 oz. egg noodles
1/2 c. cooked cracked wheat

3 T. chicken-flavored bouillon
1/2 c. chopped celery
1 c. Chicken Cheeseburger Pcs. (p. 127)
1 t. minced parsley for garnish
1/4 c. white bean flour to thicken

Combine all but cheese and parsley and cook 15-20 minutes, until noodles are tender. Mix bean flour with 1/2 c. water and stir into cooked mixture. Cook an additional 3 minutes, stirring occasionally. Add "Cheeseburger" pieces and heat through. Garnish with parsley. Serves 8.

Cal. 74 **Fat** .8g/9% **Carb.** 14g **Fbr.** 1g **Pro.** 3g

"CLAM" CHOWDER

2 qt. boiling water
2 c. shredded potatoes
1 c. shredded onions
1 1/2 c. Queso Blanco cheese

3 T. clam soup base
1 1/2 c. shredded carrots
1/2 c. white bean flour or cornstarch
2/3 c. dry milk powder

Combine water, vegetables, cheese (crumbled very fine to resemble clam pieces) and bouillon and cook 15 minutes over medium heat. Stir in cracked wheat. Mix dry milk powder and bean flour or cornstarch into 1 c. warm water. Add slowly to hot mixture and stir until well blended and thickened. Add more thickening if you like your soup creamier. Serves 6.

Cal. 187 **Fat** .3g/1.5% **Carb.** 38g **Fbr.** 6g **Pro.** 9g

CREAM OF TOMATO SOUP

4 c. water
1 t. dry minced onion
2 T. butter or margarine (opt.)
1 T. beef or chicken-flavored bouillon

2 c. tomato sauce
salt and pepper to taste
2/3 c. dry milk powder
1/4 c. cornstarch

Blend all ingredients with 2 cups of water for 1 minute. Pour into saucepan and stir while cooking over medium-high heat until thick, about 5 minutes. Serves 4.

Cal. 89 **Fat** .5g/5% **Carb.** 17g **Fbr.** 2g **Pro.** 6g

ORIENTAL VEGETABLE SOUP

4 c. boiling water	1 c. chopped celery
4 T. chicken-flavored bouillon	1 c. chopped onion
1 c. Napa cabbage	1 c. chopped green pepper
1 c. sliced mushrooms	1/2 t. ground ginger
1 T. soy sauce	1 1/2 c. cubed Queso Blanco

Add all except cabbage and bring to boil. Reduce heat and cook, covered for 10 minutes. Add cabbage and cook 5 minutes. Serve with extra soy sauce, if desired. Serves 6.

Cal. 49 **Fat** .4g/7% **Carb.** 5g **Fbr.** 2g **Pro.** 2g

ITALIAN SPAGHETTI SOUP

4 c. boiling water	1 c. broken spaghetti pieces
2 T. dry cracked wheat	

Stir spaghetti and wheat into boiling water and bring mixture back to a boil. Reduce heat and simmer, covered, 8 minutes while gathering:

1/2 t. basil	1 T. clam or chicken-flavored bouillon
1 t. parsley	2 T. olives, chopped or sliced
dash garlic powder	pepper, if desired
1 c. "Cheeseburger" Curds	

Add all to cooked spaghetti mixture. Bring to a boil, reduce heat and cook 2 minutes, covered. Ladle into bowls and sprinkle with homemade parmesan cheese.

Cal. 85 **Fat** .7g/7% **Carb.** 16g **Fbr.** .5g **Pro.** 3g

SALADS

Salads generally provide a means of incorporating lots of fresh, crunchy vegetables which are a good source of fiber. You can also add cooked grains to almost any salad recipe for increased nutrition and a double dose of fiber.

Most salads can also be used as sandwich fillings and when combined with whole grain breads, you have a complete meal.

The homemade salad dressings starting on p. 21 are very fast and easy to make and much more nutritious than commercial brands.

HOT CRAB SALAD

2 c. simmered crab pieces, (see p. 129)   1/8 t. dried basil leaves
2 c. chopped celery   1 c. fat-free mayonnaise
1 T. finely chopped onion   1 T. lemon juice
1 t. dried parsley flakes   1/2 t. salt

Add all ingredients to hot crab pieces. Serve over pasta, in crepes, flour tortillas or pita pockets, on a bed of lettuce or sprouts, or spread on toasted bread, topped with cheese, then broiled.

Cal. 1-5 **Fat** .1g/1% **Carb.** 15g **Fbr.** 1g **Pro.** 10g

PINEAPPLE COTTAGE CHEESE LOAF

2 c. fat-free cottage cheese   2 T. unflavored gelatin
3/4 c. fat-free mayonnaise   1 T. honey
1 c. chopped celery   1 15 oz. can crushed pineapple
1 4 1/2 oz. can chopped olives   1 c. yogurt sour cream, sweetened to taste

Drain pineapple and olives into small saucepan. Soften gelatin in this liquid, then heat until gelatin dissolves. Add to remaining ingredients. Pour into ring mold or 10"x5"x3" loaf pan coated with vegetable spray. Refrigerate until firm; unmold onto lettuce lined platter.

Cal. 425 **Fat** 3.9g/8% **Carb.** 61g **Fbr.** 1g **Pro.** 12g

BROWN RICE SALAD

4 c. cooked brown rice   1 4 oz. can chopped olives
1/3 c. French Dressing   2 T. chopped green onion
2 celery stalks, chopped   2 T. chopped green pepper
1/3 c. fat-free mayonnaise   1/2 t. prepared mustard
1 1/2 T. catsup   Salt and pepper to taste
3/4 c. yogurt cream cheese   1 c. cottage cheese

Mix all ingredients well. Add chopped hard cooked eggs, if desired. Garnish with tomato wedges and fresh parsley. Serves 6.

Cal. 245 **Fat** 3.4g/12% **Carb.** 43g **Fbr.** 4g **Pro.** 12g

MAIN DISH MEALS

I've been accused of cooking as if I only owned one pot, so I try to live up to my reputation. Any time I can save in the kitchen is time I can spend on one more project!

These main dishes are filled with great fiber and veggies. With the addition of a green salad, you have a complete meal! What could be easier?

NOODLES ROMANOFF

2 c. buttermilk
1 c. cottage cheese
1/4 t. pepper
1/2 t. dried parsley
8 oz. wide egg noodles

3 eggs or 6 egg whites, beaten
1/2 t. salt
1 t. Worcestershire sauce
2 T. cornstarch
1/3 c. chopped green onions

Cook noodles in 4 c. boiling water. Blend all remaining ingredients except onions until creamy, then add onions and cook over medium heat until thick, about 5 minutes. Serve over hot cooked noodles and sprinkle with Parmesan cheese. Serves 6.

Cal. 228 **Fat** 1.9g/8% **Carb.** 36g **Fbr.** 1g **Pro.** 16g

EASY CHEESY SPAGHETTI CUPS

8 oz. broken spaghetti
3 qt. boiling water
2 t. salt
2 c. yogurt or buttermilk

1/2 lb. grated cheese
1/4 c. minced onions
2 eggs or 4 egg whites
1/2 c. cooked cracked wheat

Boil spaghetti in water until tender. Drain and rinse. Combine spaghetti and cheese and spoon into muffin tins or custard cups coated with vegetable spray, filling 1/2 full. Mix remaining ingredients and pour over spaghetti. Bake at 350°F for 20-25 minutes or until set. Serves 4.

Cal. 383 **Fat** 1g/3% **Carb.** 36g **Fbr.** 1g **Pro.** 16g

CREAMY ITALIAN SPAGHETTI

1 lb. spaghetti noodles
4 eggs or 8 egg whites
1 c. cooked cracked wheat
4 T. homemade evaporated milk
1/3 c. grated parmesan cheese

1 cup fat-free mozzarella
1/2 c. imitation bacon bits
1/8 t. pepper
1/2 t. salt

Cook spaghetti according to package directions. Meanwhile, beat eggs and add milk, cheese, salt and pepper. Add to cooked, drained spaghetti and wheat. Mix well and garnish with bacon bits and parsley. Serves 4.

Cal. 276 **Fat** 2g/6% **Carb.** 48g **Fbr.** 2g **Pro.** 16g

RICE AND CHEESE CASSEROLE

2 c. cooked brown rice   1 small diced onion
1 diced green pepper   3 beaten egg whites
2 c. fat-free cottage cheese   1/2 c. water
1 T. butter or oil (opt.)   2 T. dry milk powder
1/2 c. each mushrooms and olives (opt.)

Mix all ingredients and bake at 350°F in muffin tins coated with vegetable spray for 20 minutes or 1 1/2 quart baking dish coated with vegetable spray for 45 minutes. Serves 4.

Cal. 276 **Fat** 2g/6% **Carb.** 48g **Fbr.** 2g **Pro.** 16g

ZUCCHINI-WHEAT SQUARES

4 c. grated zucchini   1 T. parsley flakes
6 egg whites   1 t. dried basil
2 green onions, chopped   2 T. Parmesan cheese
1 c. shredded fat-free cheese   1 c. cooked cracked wheat or brown rice

Place zucchini in colander and salt lightly. Let stand 15 minutes and squeeze out excess moisture. Simmer 3 minutes until tender. Add shredded cheese, parsley, green onions, basil, garlic, wheat or rice and eggs. Mix well. Place in buttered baking dish and sprinkle with Parmesan. Bake 30 minutes or until set. Cool slightly. Cut in squares. Serve hot or cold. Serves 8-10.

Cal. 253 **Fat** 2.9g/10% **Carb.** 36g **Fbr.** 1g **Pro.** 20g

QUICK SKILLET QUICHE

2 c. cooked brown rice   1/2 c. yogurt
2 T. chopped olives   1 c. fat-free cottage cheese
6 egg whites or 3 eggs   1 T. beef-flavored bouillon
2 T. chopped onion   2 T. Picante Sauce
2 T. dehydrated mushrooms   1 T. dehydrated green onions

Simmer mushrooms and onions (or use fresh) in 1/2 c. boiling water for 5 minutes. Mix in all other ingredients. Spread into an skillet coated with vegetable spray. Top with 1 c. grated mild cheese, if desired. Cover and cook over medium heat until cheese is melted. Cut into wedges and serve hot. Serves 4-6.

Cal. 130 **Fat** .9g/7% **Carb.** 19g **Fbr.** 1g **Pro.** 9g

GREAT CORNCHILADAS

1 c. chopped onions
2 T. chili powder
3/4 c. flour
1/4 t. tabasco sauce
12 corn tortillas
2 c. fresh or frozen corn

1/2 t. oregano
1/4 t. garlic salt
1 c. tomato sauce
3 1/2 c. water
l lb. grated cheese
1 c. cottage cheese

Cook onions and corn slightly in tomato sauce. Mix dry ingredients and add slowly to sauce and onions. Simmer 5 min. or until thickened. Layer sauce, tortillas, corn and cheeses in 9"x13" baking dish. Bake at 350°F until cheese melts, about 20-30 min. Serves 6.

Cal. 508 **Fat** 4.6g/8% **Carb.** 87g **Fbr.** 5g **Pro.** 34g

SPAGHETTI WITH VEGGIES AND CHEESE

6 c. water
1/2 lb. spaghetti
1 clove garlic, minced
2 small zucchini, sliced
2 green onions, chopped
1/4 lb. mushrooms
1 c. cooked cracked wheat

1 tomato, diced
1/2 t. dried basil
1/4 t. black pepper
1/8 t. salt
3 T. Parmesan cheese
2 t. dried parsley
1 c. fat-free cottage cheese

In 3-qt. saucepan, bring 6 c. salted water to a boil. Add spaghetti and cook over medium heat about 8 minutes. Drain well. In large skillet over medium-high heat, sauté garlic, green onions, zucchini and mushrooms in 1/4 cup water or broth. Add wheat, tomato, basil, salt and pepper. Cover and simmer 3-4 minutes, until zucchini is crispy-tender. Add vegetable mixture and cheeses to pasta. Mix gently and sprinkle with parsley. Serves 4.

Cal. 355 **Fat** 2.6g/7% **Carb.** 64g **Fbr.** 7g **Pro.** 20g

COMPANY DINNERS

Traditionally, special dinners are higher in fat and calories and lower in fiber than regular meals. With these guilt-free recipes, you can feel confident that you are serving a healthy meal that's sure to please.

SWISS CHEESE-STEAK

Make a double recipe of **Queso Blanco cheese.** After rinsing cheese curds in hot water, according to recipe, pinch off about 1/3 cup portions and quickly shape into 8 patties with your hands. Drop into boiling beef-flavored broth to cover and simmer 15 minutes. Drain and serve hot with **Swiss Steak Sauce.** Serves 8.

SWISS STEAK SAUCE

2 c. V-8 juice	1/8 t. allspice
1 T. sweet pepper flakes	1/8 t. fennel
1 t. chili powder	1/8 t. nutmeg
1/2 t. parsley flakes	1/4 t. powdered rosemary leaves
1/2 t. garlic powder	1/4 t. powdered basil
2 t. brown sugar	1/4 t. powdered oregano
1/4 t. black pepper	1 t. salt

Mix all ingredients and simmer, covered, 30 minutes. This sauce is even better after it is been stored in the refrigerator a few days. (The Amazing Wheat Book by LeArta Moulton, Used by Permission.)

Cal. 59 **Fat** .1g/2% **Carb.** 6g **Fbr.** .7g **Pro.** 10g

BURRITOS CON QUESO

1/2 c. chopped onion	1/2 c. Picante Sauce
1/2 c. diced green chilies	2 c. fat-free refried beans
1/4 c. chopped ripe olives	2 c. fat-free cottage cheese
	8 fat-free flour tortillas

Preheat oven to 400°. In a skillet or microwave, heat onion, green chilies and beans. Spread each tortilla with bean mixture, then add 2 T. cottage cheese and a little salsa. Roll and place, folded side down, in 9" x 12" baking dish coated with vegetable spray. Top with remaining cheese and olives. Bake 15 minutes, or until cheese bubbles. Serve with additional salsa on plates of shredded lettuce. Serves 8.

Cal. 172 **Fat** .5g/3% **Carb.** 31g **Fbr.** 3g **Pro.** 9g

MEXICAN LASAGNA

1/2 lb. lasagna noodles, cooked
2 c. cooked pinto beans, mashed
2 c. cooked, cracked wheat
2 c. mild enchilada sauce
1 T. beef-flavored bouillon
1 lg. onion, chopped
1 large tomato, chopped

1/4 t. garlic powder
1 t. cumin
1 t. chili powder
1/2 t. ea. salt and pepper
2 c. fat-free cottage cheese
Sour cream (opt.)

Mix all seasonings with enchilada sauce and heat through. In a 9" x 13" pan, layer sauce mix, noodles, beans, wheat, cheese, until all ingredients are used up. Bake at 400°F for 20-30 minutes, or just until cheese bubbles. OR, use flour tortillas and spoon hot sauce mixture, then beans, wheat and cheese. Garnish with chopped lettuce, tomato and sour cream, if desired. Serves 8.

Cal. 275 **Fat** 1.0g/3% **Carb.** 50g **Fbr.** .7g **Pro.** 10g

MOCK VEAL PARMESAN

1 recipe Cheeseburger Patties (p. 126)
1 c. white bean or wheat flour
1/2 t. salt
1/8 t. pepper

3 beaten egg whites
2 T. water
1 t. Worcestershire Sauce
1 1/2 c. fine bread or cracker crumbs

Sauce:
1 8 oz. can tomato sauce
1/8 t. black pepper
1 t. cornstarch

1/4 t. garlic powder
1/4 t. rosemary

Make very thin patties. Put flour, salt and pepper onto a dinner-size plate. In a small bowl, add egg, water and Worcestershire. On another plate, put fine bread or cracker crumbs. Dip the patties in each of the 3 mixtures, in the order listed. Brown patties on both sides in hot skillet coated with vegetable spray.

Mix sauce and spread a layer of sauce in a 9"x13" baking dish, add browned patties and top with additional sauce and cheese. Cover and cook until mixture is bubbling hot. Excellent when served with cooked egg noodles topped with some of the sauce from the patties. Serves 6.

Cal. 215 **Fat** 2.2g/9% **Carb.** 39g **Fbr.** 8g **Pro.** 14g

Page 156

TERIYAKI "BEEF" AND VEGETABLE FAJITAS

1 recipe "Cheeseburger" Patties (p. 125)
2 carrots   4 green onions, minced
1 lg. onion   4 ribs celery
3 8" zucchinis   1/2 c. vegetable or chicken broth
1 dozen fat-free flour tortillas

Sauce:

2 T. cornstarch   1/4 c. soy sauce
1 t. beef-flavored bouillon   1/4 t. powdered ginger
1 T. white vinegar   1/4 t. onion powder
2 T. honey or sugar   1/4 t. garlic powder
2 c. water

Mix sauce ingredients, add pressed "Cheeseburger" Curds, cut into strips and cook in a small saucepan over medium heat until mixture is slightly thickened, about 3 minutes. While the sauce is cooking, cut vegetables into long, thin strips and sauté in broth until crunchy/tender. Add cheese strips and enough sauce to moisten. Fill warmed tortillas with 1/2 c. of mixture, roll and serve with additional sauce on top. Serves 6.

Cal. 120 **Fat** .4g/3% **Carb.** 24g **Fbr.** 5g **Pro.** 9g - Filling and Sauce

CREPES WITH RICE AND PIMIENTO FILLING

6-8 crepes   1 c. fat-free cottage cheese
1 T. chicken-flavored bouillon   1/2 c. grated carrots
2 c. cooked brown rice   1 c. chopped green onions
1/2 c. chopped cooked pimientos   1 T. red lentil flour

In a heavy skillet coated with non-stick cooking spray, stir-fry filling ingredients for 2 minutes. Divide mixture into crepes (see p. 55 for Whole Wheat Crepes); roll up and place on serving tray.

Serve with Blender White Sauce (see p. 22) and garnish with 1/2 t. pimiento and a sprig of fresh parsley.

Cal. 145 **Fat** .7g/4% **Carb.** 26g **Fbr.** 3g **Pro.** 9g

DIPS AND SPREADS

Cheesey dips and spreads provide extra calcium and protein for a perfect snack or appetizer.

Homemade yogurt cream cheese is normally tart, but when honey is added, it turns into a fantastic spread or frosting.

Well, what are you waiting for? Bring on the "veggie dippers, chips and crackers for a delightful way to use powdered milk cheeses.*

NOTE:
Try peeled yams, thinly sliced, or cut into sticks, for an easy-to-chew carrot substitute.

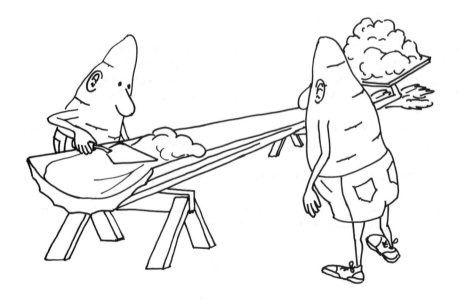

YOGURT AVOCADO DIP

1 c. fat-free yogurt
2 T. chopped ripe olives
1/4 c. fat-free mayonnaise
2 T. Picante sauce

1 avocado
1 cup cooked mashed white beans
1 T. minced chives
1/2 c. cooked cracked wheat or brown rice

Peel avocado and mix with beans until smooth, then add all ingredients and mix well. Add salt to taste. Serve chilled. Makes 2 cups.

Cal. 106 **Fat** 4.2g/37% **Carb.** 12g **Fbr.** 3g **Pro.** 4g

DOUBLE CHEESE CELERY DIP

1 c. fat-free cottage cheese
1/2 c. low-fat grated cheese
1 T. chopped green chilies
3 T. mild Picante Sauce

2 T. fat-free mayonnaise
1 t. beef-flavored bouillon
1 T. chopped green onions
1/2 c. cooked cracked wheat or brown rice

Mix all ingredients well and fill crisp ribs of celery. Makes 2 cups dip.

Cal. 95 **Fat** .3g/3% **Carb.** 13g **Fbr.** 1g **Pro.** 10g

CHEESE BALL

1 c. fat-free cottage cheese
1/2 c. fat-free grated cheese
2 T. fat-free mayonnaise
1 c. cooked cracked wheat

1 t. beef-flavored bouillon
1 T. chopped green chilies
2 T. chopped green onions
3 T. mild Picante sauce

Mix well and shape into a ball. Roll in additional chopped onions or chili powder. Chill and serve with crackers or chips. Makes 2 1/2 cups.

Cal. 41 **Fat** .1g/1% **Carb.** 5.4g **Fbr.** 9g **Pro.** 5g

Note: Homemade yogurt cream cheese spreads have a creamy texture and a tart flavor, unless combined with honey or sugar.

NUTTY CELERY SPREAD

1/4 c. fat-free cream cheese   *1/2 c. crunchy peanut butter*

Mix thoroughly and fill crunchy celery sticks. Excellent for snacks or as a salad substitute. Makes 3/4 cup.

Cal. 68 **Fat** 4.1g/45% **Carb.** 2g **Fbr.** .6g **Pro.** 3g

STRAWBERRY SPREAD

4 T. fat-free cream cheese   *4 t. honey*
1/8 t. strawberry extract   *1 t. peanut butter (optional)*

Mix well and spread on graham crackers, or beat until fluffy and use as a cake frosting. Makes 1/2 cup.

Cal. 18 **Fat** 0g/0% **Carb.** 4g **Fbr.** 0g **Pro.** 1g

PIÑA COLADA SPREAD

4 T. fat-free cream cheese   *2 T. honey*
2 T. shredded coconut   *1/2 t. vanilla*
1/4 t. each coconut and pineapple extracts

Mix well and spread on crackers or beat until fluffy and use as a frosting for cookies, cakes or muffins. Makes 1/2 cup.

Cal. 57 **Fat** .8g/13% **Carb.** 19g **Fbr.** .2g **Pro.** 2g

PEANUT BUTTER FROSTING OR FILLING

1/2 c. fat-free cream cheese   *1/2 c. peanut butter*
1/2 c. honey   *1/2 t. vanilla*
2 T. dry milk powder (opt.)

Beat well, adding dry milk powder to stiffen, if necessary. This will depend on how creamy the peanut butter is.

Cal. 87 **Fat** 4g/39% **Carb.** 11g **Fbr.** .5g **Pro.** 3g

SNACKS AND DESSERTS

These quick-to-fix snacks and desserts are a pleasure to serve, and so full of good stuff that they can be served at ANY time!

Try your hand at popsicles, fruit leather, fruit freezes, muffins and puddings. Your family will love you for your efforts and you'll love the results!

FLAVORED YOGURT

It is important to remember that as yogurt made without gelatin is stirred, it becomes more liquid. To maintain the custard consistency, stir gently or simply add flavoring as a topping. Try honey, fruit syrups, preserves, fresh or frozen fruits and granola added to yogurt.

For an individual serving:

Apple-Raisin: Mix *3 T. applesauce, 1 T. chopped raisins* and *1 t. honey and* spoon over *1 c. of set yogurt.*

Maple-Nut: Mix *1/4 t. maple extract, 1 T. chopped walnuts* and *1 t. honey* into *1 c. of set yogurt.*

Piña Colada: Mix **1 T. crushed pineapple, 1 T. shredded coconut** *and* **1 t. honey** *into* **1 c. of set yogurt.**

Pineapple-Orange: Mix *2 T. crushed pineapple* and *1 T. frozen orange juice con-centrate* into *1 c. of set yogurt.* Top with *shredded, toasted coconut,* if desired.

Fruit flavors: Add *Dole 100% frozen fruit juice concentrate* to taste.

PINEAPPLE YOGURT POPSICLES

2 c. pineapple juice　　　　　*1 c. yogurt*
3 T. honey　　　　　　　　　*1 t. vanilla*
1/4 c. dry milk powder
1 6 oz. can frozen orange juice concentrate

Blend until frothy and smooth. Freeze in small paper cups with a popsicle stick or spoon in the middle. OR, serve in dessert dishes when partially frozen to a slush. High in protein, calcium and vitamin C. Makes 4 cups mix.

Cal. 119 **Fat** .1g/1% **Carb.** 75g **Fbr.** .2g **Pro.** 3g

WHEY POPS

1 c. plain yogurt
1/2 c. dry milk powder

1 c. liquid whey
2 c. Dole Orchard Peach concentrate*

Mix thoroughly. Freeze in small paper cups with a popsicle stick or spoon in the middle. In England, the addition of whey to commercial popsicles was found to reduce tooth decay.

Cal. 69 **Fat** .1g/1% **Carb.** 14g **Fbr.** .2g **Pro.** 2g
*Note: Or use any 100% fruit juice concentrate in this recipe.

FRUIT SQUARES

1 12 oz. can Dole frozen Orchard Peach juice concentrate
1 c. plain yogurt
1/2 c. liquid whey or water

1 T. unflavored gelatin
2 T. light honey

Soften gelatin in whey or water. Bring mixture to a boil, stirring until gelatin is dissolved. Add frozen juice concentrate, then stir in remaining ingredients. Pour into 9"x13" pan coated with vegetable spray. Chill. Cut into squares when firm. Other good juices are Mountain Cherry and Country Raspberry.

Cal. 57 **Fat** .1g/1% **Carb.** 12g **Fbr.** .2g **Pro.** 1g

YOGURT SLUSH

2 c. apricot puree from fresh, bottled, or dried apricots
2 c. yogurt
Honey or sugar to sweeten

1-2 t. vanilla

Blend apricots, yogurt and vanilla, then sweeten to taste. Pour into individual serving dishes. Freeze until slushy, then serve immediately. Serves 4.

Cal. 109 **Fat** .3g/4% **Carb.** 14g **Fbr.** 2g **Pro.** 5g

PEACHY YOGURT LEATHER

4 c. peach (or apricot) puree
honey to taste

1 c. yogurt
2 T. tapioca flour

Tapioca flour (available in health food stores) thickens without cooking, so is excellent for fruit sauces and leathers.

Blend all ingredients and pour 1/2 cup at a time onto baking sheets coated with vegetable spray or dehydrator trays lined with plastic wrap in 3" circles. The circles dry faster than solid sheets and make nice individual snacks.

Cal. 43 **Fat** .1g/1% **Carb.** 9g **Fbr.** 1g **Pro.** 1g

BLENDER FRUIT FREEZE

2 c. yogurt
2 frozen peaches
1 t. vanilla

2 frozen bananas
6 oz. frozen apple juice
pinch of salt

Cut frozen fruit into chunks and add to yogurt in blender. Blend until thick and creamy. (If your blender does not have a strong motor, let frozen fruit thaw 5-10 minutes.) Serve immediately. Serves 4.

Cal. 212 **Fat** .5g/2% **Carb.** 41g **Fbr.** 2g **Pro.** 5g

CHEESE-WHEAT SNAX

4 c. cooked whole wheat kernels
2 c. grated fat-free cheese
2 T. parmesan cheese

4 T. dry onion flakes
4 t. beef-flavored bouillon

Mix all ingredients except Parmesan and grind in hand food grinder with a medium blade. Sprinkle with Parmesan cheese before spreading on baking sheet coated with vegetable spray. Dry at 150°F for 30-45 minutes, or until crunchy.

Cal. 66 **Fat** 1.1g/17% **Carb.** 8g **Fbr.** .4g **Pro.** 3g

HICKORY SNAX - Add *1 t. Liquid Smoke* to above recipe before grinding.

SOUR CREAM GINGERBREAD

2/3 c. raisins
1 c. boiling water
1/4 c. dark molasses
3 1/2 c. wheat flour
2 t. baking soda
2 t. powdered cinnamon
2 T. applesauce or canola oil

1 c. fat-free sour cream
2/3 c. honey
3 egg whites
3 T. applesauce
2 t. powdered ginger
1 t. vanilla
1 t. salt, opt.

Start oven at 400°F. Coat 2 loaf pans with vegetable spray. Pour boiling water over the raisins and let stand 5 minutes; drain and let cool. Combine the sour cream, butter, honey, molasses and eggs and beat well. Sift the flour with the salt, soda and spices. Add to the creamed mixture and beat well. Add the raisins and mix. Pour into loaf pans. Bake about 25 minutes, or until center is done.
Serves 6.

Cal. 246 **Fat** 1.6g/6% **Carb.** 53g **Fbr.** 5g **Pro.** 6g

PINEAPPLE-YOGURT NUT MUFFINS

2 1/2 c. wheat flour
1/2 c. wheat or oat bran
1 T. wheat germ
1 t. baking soda
1 t. baking powder
dash salt
1 t. lemon juice
1/2 c. chopped walnuts, opt.

1/4 c. chopped dates
1 c. raisins
1/2 c. drained pineapple
2 T. applesauce or canola oil
2 T. light molasses
3 T. honey
2 c. fat-free yogurt
2 egg whites, beaten

In a bowl, stir together all dry ingredients. Make a "nest" and add all wet ingredients except for egg whites. Stir just until moistened. Fold in egg whites. Pour into muffin tins coated with cooking spray and bake in a 375°F oven until bread tests done in the center, about 25 minutes. Serve hot or cold. Makes 1 dozen muffins.

(These are excellent served with a sauce made from 1 c. pineapple juice, 2 T. honey, 3 T. butter, 1 t. vanilla and 2 T. cornstarch. Heat until thickened.)

Cal. 196 **Fat** .7g/3% **Carb.** 43g **Fbr.** 5g **Pro.** 6g

CREAMY 3-MINUTE PUDDING

2 c. hot water
1 T. butter (opt.)
1/3 c. honey
1/3 c. dry milk powder
1/8 t. lemon extract

1 egg or 2 egg whites
1 t. vanilla
3 T. cornstarch
1/4 t. salt

Add butter (if used) and honey to 1 cup of the water and bring to a boil over medium heat. Mix remaining ingredients with remaining water until free of lumps, using blender or wire whip. Pour slowly into boiling water, stirring constantly. When thickened, about 30 seconds, stir well enough to mix in any lumps. Serve hot or cold. This is delicious topped with fresh or frozen strawberries and Graham Cracker or Grape Nuts crumbs (see Section One for recipes).

Cal. 132 **Fat** 1g/7% **Carb.** 27g **Fbr.** 1g **Pro.** 5g

VARIATIONS TO BASIC PUDDING RECIPE

COCONUT PUDDING

Add 1/4 t. coconut flavoring and if desired, sprinkle coconut on top of individual servings.

MAPLE NUT PUDDING

Omit vanilla and replace with 1/2 t. maple flavoring, or use regular recipe and drizzle maple syrup over each individual serving. Add chopped, toasted walnuts.

EGGNOG PUDDING

Use 3 eggs instead of 1. Add a dash of nutmeg and 1/4 t. liquid artificial rum flavoring.

QUICK CAROB PUDDING

1/3 c. honey
1/3 c. dry milk powder
4 eggs or 8 egg whites
1/4 t. salt
2 T. cornstarch

3 T. carob powder
2 c. water
1 T. vanilla
1 T. butter (opt.)

In a medium saucepan, heat 1 1/2 c. warm water, butter (if used) and honey. Pour 1/2 c. water into blender jar and add remaining ingredients. Blend about 1 minute and then whisk mixture into boiling water and cook over medium heat. Stir and cook about 3 minutes. Pour into individual serving dishes and refrigerate until ready to serve. Serves 4.

Cal. 194 **Fat** 1g/7% **Carb.** 35g **Fbr.** 2g **Pro.** 7g

VARIATIONS TO QUICK CAROB PUDDING RECIPE

CAROB MINT PUDDING

Add 1 t. dried spearmint leaves (or about 5 fresh spearmint leaves) to water until it boils. Then remove or strain and follow regular recipe. OR, add mint flavoring to taste.

CAROB PUDDING POPS

Add 2 T. cornstarch to basic Carob Pudding recipe. Blend and then cook until thickened, about 1 minute. Pour or spoon into a 9"x13" cake pan and freeze. When firm but not yet solid, cut into 2" squares. Push a popsicle stick into each square and freeze until solid. Re-cut if necessary.

Carob Pudding Pops can also be made in 3 oz. paper cups with a stick inserted when pudding is frozen until almost firm. To serve, peel off cup and go for it!

TAPIOCA PUDDING

Bring to a boil:

2 c. water

1/3 c. honey

2 T. quick cooking tapioca

1 T. butter (opt.)

(For faster cooking, regular tapioca can be coarsely cracked using a blender or small seed grinder.)

Combine in blender:

2 eggs or 4 egg whites

1 t. vanilla

1/2 c. of the boiling water mixture

1/4 t. salt

1/8 t. lemon extract

1/2 c. dry milk powder

Blend eggs and water first, then add remaining ingredients while blending. Pour slowly into boiling water mixture while stirring. Cook over medium-high heat about 1 minute, or until thick. Pudding should not boil. Pour into individual serving dishes and chill. Serves 4.

Cal. 151 **Fat** .1g/0% **Carb.** 32g **Fbr.** .1g **Pro.** 7g

RASPBERRY YOGURT CHEESECAKE

8" pie crust - regular or graham cracker

Filling:

1 c. yogurt cream cheese

1 egg

1 t. vanilla

1 c. cottage cheese

4 T. dry milk powder

1/3 c. honey

Blend until smooth. Pour into crust. Bake at 325°F for 25 minutes.

Topping:

1 c. yogurt sour cream

1 t. vanilla

1/2 t. lemon juice

2 T. dry milk powder

2 t. honey

Blend well. Pour over baked cheesecake. Bake at 400°F for 7-8 minutes.

Raspberry Fruit Sauce:

2 c. raspberries

1 c. light honey

1 t. lemon juice

3 c. water

4 T. cornstarch

Mix and cook over medium heat until thick. Pour over cooled cheesecake.

Cal. 190 **Fat** 1.8g/8% **Carb.** 41g **Fbr.** 2g **Pro.** 5g

INFORMATION SECTION

I've included in this section the most-often-asked questions on using and storing grains, beans, seeds, powdered milk, and other basic foods.

You'll learn ways to SNEAK nutritious foods into your family favorites, what to do if you can't tolerate wheat or milk, and why grains are such an important part of a good diet.

My family always wants to know WHY something is or is not good for them. When I supply the proper information, they are much more likely to try new foods. When my children were small, they would go to their neighborhood friends and tell them about all the Vitamin C they ate in their handful of sprouts, or that the Vitamin A in their carrots gave them x-ray vision. You might want to get a vitamin/mineral chart to show the best foods to use and help them learn the functions foods have in providing nutrients.

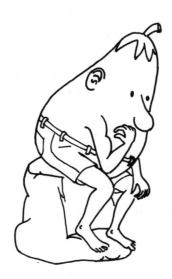

Most OFTEN-Asked Questions

Q. What do I look for in buying a mill to grind grains and beans?
A. **1)** A good guarantee, in writing! Any mill will grind grains, but some manufacturers say they will not guarantee their mill will grind beans. Any mill is bound to malfunction at one time or another, but some companies stand behind their products and others make excuses why you should be responsible for payment on expensive repairs. I have had the best customer service with the K-Tec Kitchen Mill. **2)** Look for one that mills at low temperatures to best preserve nutrients.

Q. What is the shelf life of bean and grain flours?
A. Beans and grains have a protective, full-of-fiber outer shell. Once that is broken, nutrients decrease and deterioration begins. Fresh flours should be used within 1-2 weeks or refrigerated. (Zip-loc freezer bags and wide mouth quart jars filled with bean flours freeze well and are easy to use.) Ideally, flours should be ground just before using, but that is not always possible. I have kept bean flours on the shelf for more than a year as a test. While no flavor change can usually be detected, I know that nutrients have been lost.

Q. I don't have time to cook brown rice and whole or cracked wheat before I even start preparing a meal, so I always end up using instant white rice. Help!
A. Cooked grains and beans can be frozen in 2-cup portions in quart zip-loc freezer bags for up to 6 months. I fill the bags, then flatten and press out as much air as possible. After zipping shut, I lay them flat in the freezer on a baking tray. When frozen, I stack them 6-8 high on one side of my freezer. To thaw, place the bag in a pan of warm water or defrost in the microwave.

Q. *Do I have to wash beans before grinding? I wash them before cooking, why not before grinding?*

A. Years ago, packages of dry beans from the grocery store and especially from food storage sources, used to contain rocks, small dirt clods and dust. Nowdays, beans are usually "triple cleaned." While you may find an occasional chunk of dirt, the beans themselves are usually shiny and clean. I pour 2 cups of beans at a time into the hopper of my mill and sort them as they are being ground.

Q. *How can I add fiber to fast foods? Most of the time, that's all my family will eat! Usually, they only want what comes from a can or a box.*

A. Sneak it in! Find some of their favorite foods (pizza, tacos, hamburgers) and fortify them by adding bean flours, cooked beans and grains. If you have a take-out pizza, sprinkle the top with a cup of cooked brown rice and cover it up with extra olives and cheese. If you use ground beef or ground poultry to make tacos or burgers, add 1/4 cup of bean flour and 1 cup of cooked brown rice to each cup of ground meat. Season with 2-3 t. beef or chicken bouillon or a packaged seasoning mix.

Q. *How do I keep my family from dictating what foods I prepare?*

A. Nutrition is serious business, and we have a stewardship to take the best care possible of the bodies we've been given. Parents have the responsibility to teach and train children to enjoy nutritious foods. Try having a family council and letting everyone help decide the menu for one high-fiber, super nutritious meal each week. Vary the menu and you'll come up with a good variety of family favorites. After a few months, add another "nutrition day". Gradually sneak in beans, bean flours and grains to their traditional favorites. Most people can't even tell the difference, except they are more quickly satisfied and stay full longer! That's a real plus when you're feeding teenagers!!!

Q. I tossed out all my prepared foods and started feeding my family whole wheat bread and whole-grain cereals and veggie burgers instead of hamburgers. Now they all have diarrhea and I'm in the doghouse. What can I do?

A. "Buck Up" and get used to it! No, seriously, this is a REAL problem and occurs when meals are not balanced with proper amounts of vegetables and beans. Gradually increasing the amount of whole grains is safest.

Q. Why are wheat, beans and rice considered "basic" foods?
A. Grains and legumes combine to form a complete protein. Soybeans are complete by themselves. Vegetable proteins are more readily digestible and easier for our bodies to utilize.

Q. Why are cracked grains and beans used?
A. Cracking, like cutting or grating large vegetables, speeds cooking time. See COUNTRY BEANS, for more fast ways to use bean flour, which is milled from dry beans and cooks in only 3 minutes for fast fat-free soups, sauces, gravies, and much more.

Q. Why are cracked grains, beans and wheat flour refrigerated?
A. As soon as the hard outer shell of dried grains and legumes is broken or removed, nutrients begin to deteriorate and go rancid. Freezing stops this action.

Q. Why is it so important to add grains to almost every recipe?
A. The USDA recommends 6-11 servings of grains each day. The Benson Institute (Brigham Young University, Provo, Utah 84602) research supports the USDA findings and indicates that 50-60% of calories should come from grain and grain products and legumes (beans). Most of those grains and beans should be WHOLE grains, meaning whole, cracked, or ground into flour, but not processed. Dividing your year's supply into daily portions, 300 lb. of wheat would average 5 cups of cooked or sprouted grains or flour daily! Using and storing a *variety* of grains and legumes is ESSENTIAL!

Q. What if I am allergic to wheat?
A. Thousands of people have been diagnosed with an allergy to wheat. This poses a definite problem, but there IS an answer! All recipes calling for whole or cracked wheat and many breads using baking powder or soda as a leavening agent can be altered to use rice flour or other grain flours in place of wheat flour. Health food stores usually carry alternative gluten-free flours. A recipe is included in this book to make your own gluten-free mix at home.

Q. Why aren't meat recipes included?
A. Although I am not a vegetarian and use meat occasionally, research shows that meat is not NECESSARY to obtain complete protein with proper combining of grains and vegetables and legumes. Most meats are kept frozen, a luxury we may not have in the event of widespread electrical failure.

Q. What are some good sources of protein?
A. The Benson Institute suggests that 10 to 20% of our calories should come from protein foods and the easiest to store are forti-fied dry milk, tuna fish, and beans (legumes).

Q. What kind of fats should I use?
A. Vegetable oil, shortening, peanut butter, mayonnaise, butter and margarine powders can be stored to provide the necessary 5-10% of our calories that should come from fats, according to the Benson Institute. The American diet typically consists of more than 40% fat, far more than is necessary.

Q. In desserts, crackers, pancakes, etc., that call for wheat flour, why mix ingredients ONLY until moistened?
A. Because the gluten in wheat flour is quickly developed and dough becomes tough. Very few recipes call for beating.

Q. When baking, why are honey recipes more brown?
A. Honey darkens when heated and tends to burn easily in some recipes.

Sprout Questions and Answers

Q. How many sprouts do we have to eat to get a full day's supply of vitamin C?
A. The general rule of thumb is 1/2 cup, and sprouts with leaves allowed to turn green are the highest in ALL nutrients.

Q. How do I keep sprouts from going sour or slimy?
A. Rinsing 2-3 times a day, with PROPER DRAINAGE after each rinsing will keep sprouts fresh.

Q. My husband and family say they won't eat sprouts. How can I sneak them in so they won't notice?
A. Sprouted beans look much the same as regular beans, so try soups, chili, as well as chopped sprouts in patties. If necessary, break off the sprout tails and blend them with other liquid ingredients.

Q. How long do sprouts keep in the refrigerator?
A. For optimum nutrition, sprouts store only 3-4 days, but some varieties will actually keep up to 2 weeks.

Q. Why do mung and soy sprouts turn green when I try to sprout them long?
A. The presence of light causes greening, so make sure they are kept completely in the dark.

Q. Can the "gas" from beans be eliminated?
A. Pinto and kidney beans are the most likely to cause gas. Sprouting adds enzymes that change indigestible carbohydrates to digestible carbohydrates. Even though cooking would destroy those enzymes, the carbohydrates would still be in a more usable form. Beans cooked at low temperatures would be best. Tolerance for high fiber foods, like beans and whole grains, increases when those foods are eaten often.

Q. Why aren't long mung and soy bean sprouts as white as the ones in the grocery store?
A. Commercial sprouts are often bleached, and are grown in absolute darkness. (No one peeks under the burlap to see how they are doing!)

Q. What happens to the nutrients in sprouts when they are cooked?
A. More than half of the vitamins and minerals remain after cooking, unless cooked in water that is discarded. Stir-frying or lightly steaming sprouts would result in a 20-30% loss of nutrients. If you use a variety of sprouts and include raw sprouts daily (1/2 c. per person) in salads, sandwiches, drinks, or just by the handful, then the nutrients lost in cooking will not be significant.

Q. How can I be sure my family is getting enough vitamins?
A. Beans and grains are often low in vitamins A, C, and D, all of which can be obtained by growing and using fresh fruits and vegetables and sprouts. Alfalfa, wheat, sunflower, soy and mung beans are the most versatile.

Sprouts can take the place of bottled fruits and vegetables in providing bulk as well as nutrients. Remember, many valuable nutrients are lost in cooking, so collect a variety of good tasting recipes your family enjoys using uncooked sprouts.

Q. What if I can't tolerate milk?
A. If you can't drink milk, store sunflower and sesame seeds, nuts and soybeans to sprout. Calcium is present in nearly all foods in small quantities, especially dark green, leafy vegetables and sprouts allowed to "green" in the sun (like alfalfa, sunflower, buckwheat, clover and radish). See 1-2-3 Smoothies by Rita Bingham for recipes to make "milk" from grains, nuts and seeds.

Q. What other grains and seeds can be sprouted?
A. Anything capable of growing can be sprouted and eaten, but you must be careful not to use seeds treated with pesticides for use in gardening. They are POISON. Usually, (but not always) a pink dye has been added to treated seeds as a warning.

Cheese Questions and Answers

Q. Can cheese be stored?
A. Yes, it can be frozen or wrapped in vinegar soaked cloth or paraffin and stored in a cool place. Several varieties can easily be made from powdered milk. Most cheeses can be made in only 3 minutes(!!!) using newly developed techniques.

Q. What acids can be used to curdle milk?
A. Any acid will curdle milk. The best tasting cheeses are made with rennet, fresh lemon juice, reconstituted lemon juice, white vinegar and ascorbic acid.

Q. If cheeses are just made with dry milk, water and an acid, will they taste good by themselves?
A. You can add buttermilk, salt and other flavorings (see below), but I most often use the dry cheese curds in salads, sandwich fillings, patties and casseroles. They are meant to add protein, not to add flavor.

Q. What seasonings can I use to flavor homemade cheeses?
A. Salt, onion and garlic salt, seasoned salts, parsley, chives, sesame seeds, caraway seeds, green chilies, hot peppers, olives, pimiento and buttermilk. If you mix these cheeses with commercial cheese and use in a recipe, most people will never be able to tell the difference.

Q. What if I only have instant milk? Can I use that in your recipes?
A. Instant crystals are fluffier than non-instant powder, but they can be blended to a powder, then used in any of my recipes. When making milk, 3 cups of non-instant powdered milk makes 1 gallon of liquid milk.

BASIC INGREDIENT SHOPPING LIST

- ❑ apple juice
- ❑ applesauce
- ❑ ascorbic acid powder
- ❑ beans
- ❑ bottled or fresh mushrooms
- ❑ bran
- ❑ brown rice
- ❑ brown sugar
- ❑ butter
- ❑ buttermilk
- ❑ canola oil
- ❑ carob chips
- ❑ carob powder
- ❑ catsup
- ❑ cheese coloring (opt.)
- ❑ chopped olives
- ❑ clam bouillon
- ❑ coconut
- ❑ corn tortillas
- ❑ cornmeal
- ❑ cornstarch
- ❑ cottage cheese
- ❑ cream cheese
- ❑ dry milk powder
- ❑ dry minced onion
- ❑ eggs
- ❑ enchilada sauce
- ❑ fat-free cottage cheese
- ❑ fat-free mayonnaise
- ❑ flour tortillas
- ❑ freeze-dried yogurt starter

- ❑ fresh fruit
- ❑ fresh fruit juices
- ❑ fresh or bottled lemon juice
- ❑ fresh vegetables
- ❑ frozen concentrated fruit
- ❑ gelatin, unflavored
- ❑ grated orange peel
- ❑ green chilies
- ❑ honey
- ❑ hot pepper sauce
- ❑ imitation bacon bits
- ❑ juices
- ❑ junket rennet tablets
- ❑ Kitchen Bouquet
- ❑ lasagne noodles
- ❑ lemon juice
- ❑ lentils
- ❑ liquid smoke
- ❑ liquid whey from yogurt
- ❑ low-fat grated cheese
- ❑ malted milk
- ❑ millet
- ❑ molasses
- ❑ mustard
- ❑ nuts
- ❑ oat bran
- ❑ oatmeal
- ❑ oats, whole
- ❑ olive oil
- ❑ onions
- ❑ parmesan cheese

SHOPPING LIST (Cont'd)

- ❑ pasta
- ❑ peach pureé
- ❑ pasta
- ❑ peanut butter
- ❑ peas
- ❑ Picante sauce (Pace's)
- ❑ pineapple
- ❑ powdered yogurt starter
- ❑ raisins
- ❑ refried beans
- ❑ sesame seeds
- ❑ shredded coconut
- ❑ spaghetti sauce (homemade)
- ❑ soy sauce
- ❑ sunflower seeds
- ❑ taco sauce

- ❑ tapioca
- ❑ tapioca starch
- ❑ tomato paste
- ❑ tomato sauce
- ❑ tomatoes
- ❑ tuna packed in water
- ❑ vegetable bouillon
- ❑ V-8 juice
- ❑ wheat bran
- ❑ wheat germ
- ❑ wheat
- ❑ white flour
- ❑ white vinegar
- ❑ whole wheat
- ❑ Worcestershire sauce
- ❑ yogurt

Spices

- ❑ basil
- ❑ BBQ seasoning
- ❑ black pepper
- ❑ cayenne pepper
- ❑ chili powder
- ❑ cinnamon
- ❑ curry powder

- ❑ cumin
- ❑ garlic powder
- ❑ ginger
- ❑ marjoram
- ❑ nutmeg
- ❑ onion powder
- ❑ oregano

- ❑ parsley
- ❑ pepper
- ❑ sage
- ❑ salt
- ❑ sausage seasoning
- ❑ taco seasoning
- ❑ thyme

Flavorings

- ❑ vanilla extract
- ❑ cherry extract

- ❑ pineapple extract
- ❑ coconut extract

- ❑ lemon extract
- ❑ maple extract

Glossary

Bran, Flaked - The outer hull of the whole grain (wheat or oats) which is removed in the process of making white flour. A great source of fiber.

Brown Rice - Unlike most whole grains with the bran and germ intact, brown rice will go rancid within 1-2 months unless refrigerated. There are over a thousand different varieties of cultivated rice, so experiment with the ones available to you to find your favorites. Basmati brown rice is our all-time family favorite, even for those who thought they only loved white rice.

Bulgur - Whole wheat that has been boiled, dried, then cracked. Cooks in about the same time as cracked wheat.

Buckwheat - Generally used in the flour form in specialty pancake mixes, sprouted buckwheat makes a delicious lettuce substitute.

Canola Oil - A readily available vegetable made from rapeseed. It contains the lowest amounts of saturated fat.

Carob - A healthy alternative to chocolate that does NOT contain caffein. It can be found in powdered or bar form at health stores, candy shops and some grocery stores.

Cracked Wheat - Wheat cracked at home cooks in only 15 minutes. It often contains very fine particles and flour that needs to be sifted out. The resulting products can be used in cereal and in baking.

Farina - The fine particles created when wheat is cracked at home. Makes a cereal like Cream of Wheat®.

Gluten - The isolated protein part of wheat. After wheat is ground into flour, the gluten can be separated from the other components by a stirring an rinsing process. The resulting gluten is a stretchy, elastic-like product that is insoluble in water and can take on various textures when prepared with certain techniques.

Gluten Flour - gluten which has been dried and ground to a flour. Produces instant gluten when water is added.

Instant Powdered Milk - Dehydrated milk in a granular form. Sold in non-fat or full-fat varieties. Shorter shelf life than Non-Instant.

Millet - Alias birdseed, without the outer hull. It is one of the oldest grains and is excellent served as a cereal or pilaf. Millet's mild flavor and easy digestability make this grain a #1 good choice for baby cereal.

Non-Fat Dry Milk Powder - Dehydrated milk in a powdered form. May be either instant or non-instant (which is usually cheaper).

Nuts - Much of the fat from nuts sold commercially comes from the added fat used in processing them. When eaten raw (after 4 hours of soaking), the natural enzymes in nuts work to help digest the fats they contain. They are then easily digested, and very filling, especially in a fruity breakfast Smoothie. Nuts can be ground to a meal and sprinkled on cereals, or on pancakes. Shelled nuts should always be refrigerated. Almonds have the least fat.

(Junket) Rennet Tablets - Rennet makes excellent 3-minute cheeses. Look for a small box, in the "jello" aisle. Usually used to make homemade ice cream. To order, call Redco Foods at 1-800-556-6674.

Seasoned Rice Vinegar - Similar to Balsamic Vinegar, but lighter in color. Some rice vinegars are "brewed" so long that they turn to wine and are labeled "Rice Wine Vinegar." I prefer to buy the brands that do not contain alcohol.

Sesame Oil - Found in the Oriental Seasoning section of your grocery store, this <u>dark</u> oil is pressed from toasted sesame seeds. Just a few drops flavors a whole bowl of rice or pasta! Use sparingly. (Light sesame oil is also available, but isn't as flavorful.)

Sesame Seeds - Tiny seeds packed with calcium. Tahini, ground sesame seeds, is used in place of or can be mixed with peanut butter. Brown sesame seeds are unhulled and require more chewing.

Hulled white sesame seeds are more readily available and are preferred when making sesame "milk" for use in breakfast shakes. Toasted seeds are excellent over Chinese dishes and salads.

Soybeans - The only legume that contains all 8 essential amino acids for a complete protein. Also high in calcium. Used as a coarsely cracked grain (grits), as a flour, soymilk and tofu.

Soy Sauce - Fermented soybean juice. Tamari sauce is the only variety without MSG and preservatives. Great for seasoning gravies, casseroles, rice, and millet.

Sucanat® - Evaporated cane juice, granulated; contains all the vitamins and minerals of cane juice. Manufactured by NutraCane, Inc., 5 Meadowbrook Parkway, Milford, NH 03055.

Sunflower Seeds - Whole seeds, raw or toasted, seasoned or plain, make a great high protein snack. Ground seeds make a meal that can be added to breads, cereals and nut-butters. Sprouted sunflower seeds make an excellent lettuce replacement in salads or sandwiches.

Tofu - The curd from soy milk, made like cheese curd from cow's milk. Bland-tasting, but very versatile. It can be sliced, cubed or blended and used in place of meat and cheese...without the saturated fat and cholesterol from dairy products.

Vegetable Broth and Bouillon- Even though I have several favorite meat-based bouillons, I prefer SOUPerior Bean's vegetarian broths. They come in chicken-, beef-, and vegetable-flavors. All are meat-free. To order, call 1-800-878-7687, or contact Duane Rough at the company's headquarters, P. O. Box 753, Brush Prairie, WA 98606.

Yeast - Recently, instant yeast has become popular, but most recipes calling for whole grain flours turn out better using regular active dry yeast. These flours contain more "heavy" bran and fiber than refined flours and take longer to rise successfully.

Dry Measures

Apples	1 lb. (3 apples)	= 3 c. sliced
Beans, dry	2 c. (1 lb.) uncooked	= 6 c. cooked
Butter	4 oz. (1 stick)	= 1/2 c. (8 T.)
Carob or Chocolate	1 lb.	= 1 c. melted
Celery	2 stalks, chopped	= 1 c.
Cheese, grated	1 lb.	= 4 c.
Cheese, grated	4 oz.	= 1 c.
Coconut, flaked	3 oz.	= 1 c.
Dates, chopped	8 oz.	= 1 c.
Dates, pitted, whole	1 lb.	= 1 1/2 c.
Eggs, whole*	3 medium or 2 large	= 1/2 c.
Egg whites	2 medium	= 1 whole egg
Flour, whole wheat	1 lb.	= 3 1/2 c.
Lemon juice	1 lemon	= 2-3 T.
Lemon rind	1 lemon, grated	= 1 1/2 t.
Macaroni	1 1/4 c. (4 oz.)	= 2 1/4 c. cooked
Nuts, whole	1 lb. shelled	= 4 c.
Nuts, chopped	5 oz.	= 1 c.
Onion, medium	1 chopped	= 1/2 c.
Orange juice	1 orange	= 1/2 c.
Orange rind	1 orange, grated	= 1 T.
Raisins	1 lb.	= 3 1/4 c.
Rice	1 c. uncooked	= 3 1/2 c. cooked
Yeast	1 packet	= 1 T.

*Note: 1 egg has the leavening power of 1/2 tsp. baking powder

Abbreviations and Measurements

dash	=	less than 1/8 teaspoon (t.)
1 teaspoon (t)	=	1/8 fluid ounce
3 t.	=	1 tablespoon (T.)
2 Tablespoons (T.)	=	1/8 cup (c.)
4 T.	=	1/4 c.
8 T.	=	1/2 c.
12 T.	=	3/4 c.
16 T.	=	1 c.
1 cup (c.)	=	1/2 pint (pt.)
1 pint (pt.)	=	2 c. (16 oz.)
1 quart (qt.)	=	2 pts. (4 c.)
1 gallon (gal.)	=	4 quarts (qts.)
16 oz.	=	1 pound (lb.)

Substitutions

If you don't have this...	Use this instead:
1 t. baking powder	1/4 t. soda + 1 t. cream of tartar
1 c. butter	1 c. canola oil
1 c. corn syrup	1 c. honey
1 egg, whole	2 egg whites or 2 egg yolks
1 T. wheat flour (for thickening)	1 T. bean flour or 1 1/2 t. cornstarch
2 c. cake flour	1 3/4 c. wheat flour + 2 T. cornstarch
1 clove garlic	1/8 t. garlic powder
1 c. whole milk	1/4 c. non-instant dry milk + 1 c. water
1 c. sour milk/ buttermilk	1 c. fresh milk + 1 T. lemon juice or vinegar
1 c. sour cream	Blend 1 c. cottage cheese, 2 T. buttermilk and 1 t. lemon juice
1 t. dry mustard	1 t. prepared mustard
1 onion, small	3 T. instant minced onion

Recommended Storage Times
Cupboard Storage

BAKING PRODUCTS	RECOMMENDED STORAGE TIME	HANDLING SUGGESTIONS
Baking powder	6 months	*Store all baking products*
Baking soda	10 months	*tightly covered in a cool,*
Corn meal	3 months	*dry place*
Flour	1 month	
Cracked grains	1 month	
Grain and bean flours	1 month	
Pancake mix	3 to 6 months	
Muffin mix	3 to 6 months	
Cooking oil	6 months	
Olive oil	indefinitely	
Spices and herbs	6 months	*Store in a dark place*
Vanilla	12 months	

CONDIMENTS		
Bottled salad dressings	6 months	*Unopened or refrigerated*
Catsup	12 months	
Mustard	12 months	
Mayonnaise	3 to 6 months	
Peanut butter	6 to 9 months	

CEREALS		
Whole grains	6 to 12 months	*Store all cereal grains*
Cracked grains	1 month	*tightly covered in a cool,*
Oatmeal	1 month	*dry place*

MISCELLANEOUS		
Bread	2-4 days	*Store tightly covered in a cool, dry place*
Canned beans	2 years	
Nonfat dry milk	2 years, unopened	*Opened milk stays fresh for 6 months in an airtight container.*

Recommended Storage Times
Freezer Storage

DAIRY PRODUCTS	RECOMMENDED STORAGE TIME	HANDLING SUGGESTIONS
Butter	6 to 9 months	*Place in zip-loc freezer bags*
Hard Cheeses	4 to 6 months	*Place in zip-loc freezer bags*
FRUITS AND VEGGIES		
All varieties - fresh	8 to 12 months	*Place in zip-loc freezer bags*
All varieties - frozen	8 to 12 months	*Store in original package*
PREPARED FOODS		
Cooked or Sprouted Beans and Grains	3 to 6 months	*Place in zip-loc freezer bags*
Patties and loaves	1 to 2 months	*Place in zip-loc freezer bags*
Breads	2 to 3 months	*Place in zip-loc freezer bags*
Soups, Stews	4 to 6 months	*Place in airtight plastic containers*

Refrigerator Storage

DAIRY PRODUCTS	STORAGE TIME	SUGGESTIONS
Butter	1 to 2 months	*Store in original package*
Hard Cheeses	3-4 weeks	*Store in original package*
Soft Cheeses	1 week - homemade	*Store in airtight container*
	1 week past sell date	*Store in original package*
Milk	1 week for mixed	*Store in airtight container*
	1 week past sell date	*Store in original package*
Yogurt	1 week - homemade	*Store in airtight container*
	1 week past sell date	*Store in original package*
Eggs (in shell)	4-5 weeks	*Store in original package*
Egg yolks	1 week	*Store in airtight container*

Grinding Beans to a Flour

When added to boiling water, bean flours thicken in only 1 minute, and in 3 minutes are ready to eat. Bean flours added to baked goods increase vitamins and minerals and provide a source of complete protein.

Modern equipment for the kitchen has revolutionized the use of beans! Dry beans can be ground to a fine flour using a hand grinder for small quantities, or electric mills for larger quantities. Bean flour stores well and is great to have on hand for "instant" soups, sauces, dips, sandwich fillings and gravies, and to add to almost everything you cook or bake. (Even though these flours appear to store well at room temperature, any flour will retain more nutrients if refrigerated or frozen.)

There are at least 2 electric home mills which are guaranteed to grind all types of grains and beans to a fine flour. These are the K-Tec Kitchen Mill (1-800-748-5400), and the GrainMaster Whisper Mill (801) 263-8900. The Back To Basics hand mill (1-800-688-1989) will also grind grains and beans to a flour, although not quite as fine. Mills with grinding stones must be cleaned after each 2 cups of beans by grinding 1 cup of hard wheat. Do not grind soy beans if your mill uses grinding stones. If beans are too large to go easily into the grinding chamber of your electric mill, crack first with a blender or hand grain cracker.

Sort beans, checking for broken, dirty beans or rock pieces. (Most beans nowadays have been "triple cleaned," making this step unnecessary.) Pour into hopper of your mill. I like to place the mill in my kitchen sink to eliminate most of the bean dust from grinding. Set mill to grind on medium-fine. The resulting flour should be as fine as the wheat flour used in baking breads, cookies, etc. (A small electric seed or coffee mill, or heavy-duty blender can be used, but will produce a more coarse flour.) Turn on mill and begin (if necessary) stirring beans (with the handle of a spoon) where they go into the grinding chamber so they will not get stuck. This is not necessary in some mills or for smaller beans and for peas and lentils. Sponge filter should be cleaned after each 2 cups of beans in the K-Tec. (Or, keep an extra filter on hand.) If flour dust is being thrown from mill, cover mill with a large kitchen towel, leaving a small opening for stirring beans.

Beans which have absorbed excess moisture will cause caking on electric mill parts. Thoroughly brush away flour residue from mill after each use. (I like to use a clean, stiff paint brush.) Then run 1 cup of dry grain through the mill to clean out internal parts. Store flour in an air tight container, preferably in the refrigerator if not used within several weeks.

PUBLICATIONS WORTH ORDERING

Natural Meals Publishing • 1-888-232-6706
www.naturalmeals.com
E-mail - info@naturalmeals.com • sales@naturalmeals.com

COUNTRY BEANS *Rita Bingham*

Nearly 400 quick, easy meatless bean recipes with over 110 bean flour recipes, including FAST, fat-free 3-minute bean soups and 5-minute bean dips. Most recipes are wheat-free, gluten-free, and dairy-free. Recipes GUARANTEED to change the way you use beans! **$14.95**

1-2-3 SMOOTHIES *Rita Bingham*

123 Quick Frosty Drinks - Delicious AND Nutritious! These energy-boosting, nutritious drinks are the best healthy treats ever! 100% natural ingredients - no sugar, preservatives, or artificial sweeteners. **$14.95**

QUICK WHOLESOME FOODS video & recipe booklet *Bingham, Moulton*

100% whole wheat breads, gluten, grains, non-fat 3-minute cheeses, sprouting and beans, 3-minute bean soups and cream sauces. Seasoning ideas for meat substitutes. Delicious, nutritious, vegetarian meals in 30 minutes or less in five 15-minute mini-classes. 65 minutes. **$29.95**

FOOD COMBINING *Rita Bingham*

Better Health—The Natural Way. Take **charge** of your health. Learn how to combine the best foods on earth—Fruits, Vegetables, Grains, Legumes, Nuts and Seeds—for best digestion, increased energy and improved health. **$7.95**

PASSPORT TO SURVIVAL *Rita Bingham and Esther Dickey*

12 Steps To Self-Sufficient Living. How to survive natural, man-made, or personal disasters. Twelve easy steps to becoming self-sufficient, including heart-smart recipes to put you on the road to better health. Learn what to store and why, where to store, and how to use what you store on a daily basis. **Design your own food storage program.** **$15.95**

Please add $3.50 shipping for 1st item, 50¢ for each additional item.

EQUIPMENT AND SUPPLIES

BOB'S RED MILL, 5209 S. E. International Way, Milwaukie, OR 97222. (503) 654-3215. Bean, pea and lentil flours, whole grains and whole grain products, books and equipment. Call or write for a mail-order catalog or nearby supplier.

COLUMBIA BEAN AND PRODUCE, INC., P. O. Box 122, Moses Lake, WA 98837. 1-800-411-2167. An excellent source for triple clean beans.

COUNTRY STORE, 9336 NE 76th Street, Vancouver, WA 98662 (360) 256-9131. Mills, mixers, all kinds of cooking equipment, books, videos, and a wide variety of canned storage foods. Walk-in or mail order. Write or call for a catalog.

ECHO HILL COUNTRY STORE, RD1, Box 1029, Fleetwood, PA 19522. (610) 944-7358. Fascinating Amish store supplying a wide variety of products, including bean, pea and lentil flours, bulk foods, cooking & baking supplies, books, quick mixes.

EMERGENCY ESSENTIALS, 165 S. Mountain Way, Orem, UT 84058. 1-800-999-1863. 72-hour kits; camping, emergency and storage supplies, equipment, containers; preparedness books and videos, foods, water purifiers, tents, backpack foods. Hand and electric mills.

FOUR STAR FOODS, Hillsboro, OR, packager of storable food reserves for emergencies, cabins, or daily use. 1-503-648-9370. Emphasis on whole grain products and quick-cooking bean and pea flours. Balanced food storage units with dehydrated fruits, vegetables, and dairy items.

HILL'S PANTRY Bosch Kitchen Center, 1269 2nd Avenue South, Lethbridge, Alberta, T1J1K5 1-403-329-8227. Hand and electric grain mills, dehydrators, juicers, home storage foods, spices, stainless steel cookware and pressure cookers.

K-TEC, Orem, UT, manufacturer of Kitchen Mill and Champ Bread Mixer (with great heavy duty blender). 1-800-748-5400. Electric mill is guaranteed to grind all beans and grains. Autoknead feature on Champ Mixer turns mixer off when bread is ready for pans - usually only 3 to 5 minutes!

LIFE SPROUTS, 745 W. 8300 S., Paradise, UT 84328. 1-800-241-1516. An excellent source for sprouters, sprouting seeds and storage containers. Their seed mixes are specially combined to provide complete nutrition.

STILLWATER RANCH P. O. Box 493583, Redding, CA 96049-3583. 1-800-429-1856. www.survivalfoods.com. Excellent source of high quality foods for long-term storage. Dehydrated foods, including powdered honey, and molasses.

WALTON FEED, INC, P. O. Box 307, Montpelier, ID 83254. 1-800-847-0465. Beans, grains, equipment, books, videos, containers, dehydrated foods, seeds, 72-hour kits. Hand and electric grain mills for cracking or grinding to a flour.

Alphabetical Recipe Index